A Wisp of Wisdom:
Animal Tales from Cameroon

Told by:

Lucy Christopher ❋ Abi Elphinstone ❋ Adèle Geras ❋ Elizabeth Laird ❋ Sarah Lean ❋ Gill Lewis ❋ Geraldine McCaughrean ❋ Tom Moorhouse ❋ Beverley Naidoo ❋ Ifeoma Onyefulu ❋ Piers Torday

Illustrated by:

Emmie van Biervliet

First published in the United Kingdom in 2016 by
Lantana Publishing Ltd., London.

'Why there is Still Enough Wisdom on Earth' © Geraldine McCaughrean 2016
'How the Tortoise Earns the Dents in his Shell' © Abi Elphinstone 2016
'Why the Dog and the Drill Monkey are Enemies' © Adèle Geras 2016
'Why it is Believed Tortoises Live Forever' © Ifeoma Onyefulu 2016
'Why the Hornbill Calls After Monkeys' © Sarah Lean 2016
'Why the Bush Pig Digs Roots from the Ground' © Tom Moorhouse 2016
'How the Fly Defeats the Elephant' © Geraldine McCaughrean 2016
'Why the Drill Monkey has a Blue Bottom' © Beverley Naidoo 2016
'How the Monkey Defeats the Crocodile' © Piers Torday 2016
'Why the Francolin's Legs are Red' © Elizabeth Laird 2016
'Why the Rat-Mole Stores Groundnuts' © Lucy Christopher 2016
'Why the Tortoise Eats Mushrooms' © Gill Lewis 2016

Illustration © Emmie van Biervliet 2016

The moral rights of the authors and illustrator have been asserted.

All rights reserved. No part of this publication may be reproduced, stored in a retrieval system, or transmitted in any form or by any means, electronic, mechanical, photocopying, recording or otherwise, without the prior written permission of the copyright owner.

ISBN-13: 978-1-911373-06-3

A CIP catalogue record for this book is available from the British Library.
Printed in the EU.

This book can be ordered directly from the publishers from the website:
www.lantanapublishing.com

CONTENTS

1. **Why there is Still Enough Wisdom on Earth**
Geraldine McCaughrean   8

2. **How the Tortoise Earns the Dents in his Shell**
Abi Elphinstone   14

9. **Why the Dog and the Drill Monkey are Enemies**
Adèle Geras   30

3. **Why it is Believed Tortoises Live Forever**
Ifeoma Onyefulu   42

7. **Why the Hornbill Calls After Monkeys**
Sarah Lean   52

10. **Why the Bush Pig Digs Roots from the Ground**
Tom Moorhouse   66

6. **How the Fly Defeats the Elephant**
Geraldine McCaughrean   80

4. **Why the Drill Monkey has a Blue Bottom**
Beverley Naidoo   88

8. **How the Monkey Defeats the Crocodile**
Piers Torday   100

5. **Why the Francolin's Legs are Red**
Elizabeth Laird   118

11. **Why the Rat-Mole Stores Groundnuts**
Lucy Christopher   126

12. **Why the Tortoise Eats Mushrooms**
Gill Lewis   140

FOREWORD

The loss of traditional knowledge from our rich natural and cultural heritage in recent years has affected our entire community. We are therefore glad that our participation in compiling these folk tales from the Korup region of Cameroon has produced a treasured book of local stories for our children and households.

Considering the importance of education for our children and the challenge of having books that reflect our local reality, this noble initiative is highly welcome as it will provide not only a book for school children to read but also a source of awareness for all. It will therefore remain a legacy for our region.

We therefore endorse this publication and pledge our continuous support to this initiative, and we shall gladly participate in distributing copies of the book to households in our community.

HRH. Chief Nganya Emmanuel
Paramount Chief of Mundemba Area

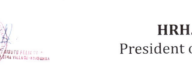

HRH. Chief Dibutu Felix Okia
President of Bima Chiefs Conference

HRH. Chief Orume III Victor Tiko
Retired Educationist & Traditional Ruler of Mokango Bima village

HRH. Chief Inyang Zachary
Senior Educationist & Traditional Ruler of Ekon 1, Korup Tribe

Why there is Still Enough Wisdom on Earth

Geraldine McCaughrean

What? You don't believe me? I'm telling you: tortoises can climb trees. At least, they could in the old days. At least, ONE tortoise certainly thought he could. At least, one tortoise tried.

In those days, tortoises looked rather different from today. They were skinny, naked little things and their feet were the biggest thing about them. With his flat head and smirky mouth, Pa Tortoise did not look very bright, but they say you should never judge anyone by the way they look. They say, too, that tortoises are clever, and this one certainly thought so. In fact, this one decided to become the wisest animal in the world.

Now, he could have gone to school, but when did you ever see a tortoise in school uniform? He could have read all the books on all the shelves in the world. But books are hard to come by in the jungle and his feet were not made for turning pages. He could have sat at the feet of the old animals and listened to all they had learned in their long, long lives. But no.

Tortoise did not just want to be wise. He wanted to own all the wisdom in the world, and to keep it to himself. So he set off around the world to collect every wisp of wisdom, every clump of cleverness, every lick of learning. He took along a big old hollow plant called a calabash to carry all his wisdom home in. It hung down from his neck on a piece of string. Like a bib.

As he walked (and tortoises walk quite slowly), he thought to himself: *When I am the One and Only Wise One, everyone will come to me for advice. They will ask me*:

"What is my name?"
"How many ants make five?"
"Where does the sun go at night?"
"Are these my teeth?"
"Who put salt in the sea?"
"Why are trees blue?"

And I shall be able to tell them. I will be the One and Only One who can tell them, because I shall have all the wisdom in the world.

On and on around the world he walked. It is a long journey to make on little legs. He grew old and toothless on the way. And as he went, he thought: *When I am the One and Only Wise One, I shall open a shop and sell advice. The other animals will make me rich. In fact, the other animals will probably make me King! And they will fetch their children along to see me, and say,* "There is the Great Wise Tortoise who Knows Things."

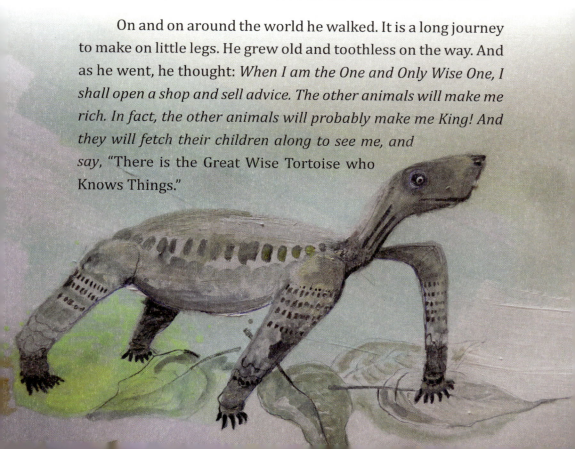

A little here, a little there, Tortoise gathered up the wisdom in every district and country and empire in the world…well, all the way from Lake Ejagham to the Rumpi Hills, anyway.

The string made his neck sore. He did not stop to LEARN any of the wisdom inside: his little head was already quite full enough with his Grand Plan. And when he had every last scrap of wisdom in his calabash, he sat down at the edge of the road and wondered where to keep his marvellous treasure. He thought and thought, and the thoughts jumped about inside his small flat skull and banged themselves on the ceiling.

"I know!" cried the One and Only Wise One. "I shall hang this calabash on the topmost twig at the topmost tip of the tallest tree in the forest. I shall sit up there like a king, halfway between the ground and the sky, and I shall see all five corners of the square world. I shall see the crowds of animals trooping towards me to ask my help to solve their problems and answer their questions, because I am so wise. And they will all be carrying presents…"

Along the thick tree roots climbed the tortoise until he came to the trunk. The bark was very rough. Tortoise's round, stumpy feet patted and pushed and poked. His gummy gums and hard mouth grasped strands of liana. But the big, round calabash hanging down in front of him (like a bib) got in the way most dreadfully. Time and again he fell on his skinny back and had to start all over again.

Rickety-rattle. Along came a pangolin. "Why, I thought tortoises were supposed to be wise. Not you, plainly!" said Pa Pangolin. "Why don't you carry that calabash on your back rather than on your belly? It would be a lot easier."

Tortoise blinked at him with bulging, blinky eyes. Pa Pangolin shrugged, and shuffled on his way: *Rickety-rattle-clatter*.

Tortoise tried again to climb the tree, but the calabash hanging down in front of him (like a bib) meant that his big stumpy feet and short little legs could not reach to grip, and he fell backwards again onto his skinny little spine.

One single thought buzzed about inside his small, flat skull: *I have NOT collected all the wisdom on earth! That pangolin still knows more than I do! Plainly I am NOT the One and Only Wise One!*

And the thought made Tortoise so angry that he took off the calabash, swung it round by its loop of string, and smashed it against the tallest tree in the forest. It crazed and cracked. Out tumbled all the wisdom in the world…well, Tortoise did not see it go exactly, but when his temper cooled and he looked inside the smashed shell of the calabash, there was nothing in there.

Not a spark, not a glow, not a word.

Gallopy-bellow-swish-grunt-hiss-hoot-skitter-plop.

The forest seemed suddenly full of the noise of other animals. He did not want them to see him. So Tortoise crept into the broken calabash and hid till night-time. In fact, he stayed in there most of the time after that and only took it off to go swimming. That's probably the best idea the One and Only Wise Tortoise ever had. Nowadays, all the tortoises are wise enough to go about in shells and you will have to be very clever if you want to catch one without his clothes on.

All the wisdom he had collected must have spread out again through the world. I expect the ants carried it, the wind blew it, the birds flew with it, the squirrels buried it, the rivers washed it away to the sea, the sun drew it up into the clouds and let it fall in the raindrops. And so, little by little, it was shared out again among the people and animals, the insects and the fish...

Just as it was meant to be.

How the Tortoise Earns the Dents in his Shell

Abi Elphinstone

One day, the animals had a conference in the sky. Yes, you heard me right: they had a conference in the sky. You see, conferences are boring at the best of times and the Korup animals felt that if they *had* to have one (which they did every year to ensure that all the animals were happy with their homes and had enough to eat), they might as well have it somewhere exciting.

And so, at dawn one morning, while most of the animals slept, Ma Elephant made her way to the top of Mount Yuhan. She stood very still for a moment as she breathed in a great lungful of air, then, with a flap of her giant ears, she let it blare out across Korup. The sound coursed through the crown trees and echoed through the caves in the forest, and then one by one, animals answered her call.

First came Ma Leopard, yellow eyes glowing in the half-light, her body slinking close to the undergrowth. She dipped her head at Elephant as she approached.

Then came Pa Civet, an explosion of black and white fur. "What did I miss? Who's here? When do we leave?" he yapped.

Before Elephant could answer, there was a flap of dark feathers and Pa Hornbill settled himself on the ground beside

Leopard. He opened his large hooked beak and gave a shaky moan. Everyone knew that Hornbill was terrified of the conference in the sky – not because of the discussions that took place up there, but because he was petrified of heights. Flying was rationed to a few flaps a day (just witnessed) and, as for soaring up into the clouds, well, that was enough to put him in bed for a month.

The animals watched as the sun rose above the horizon, casting a pale pink glow over the mountainside before disappearing behind a cloud.

Elephant peered downhill into the trees. "Come on, Pa Tortoise! The sun's already up. You're late!"

Tortoise, who was a vain little fellow, had spent the entire night admiring his reflection and was still doing so when Elephant called him. For, in those days, tortoises had smooth shells on their backs, like the curved surface of a calabash, and Tortoise was very fond of craning his neck out as far as it would go so that he could gaze at himself in his shell.

"Sorry I'm late!" he called. "I worked through the night building a new shelter for my wife and children. I've only just finished it!"

Elephant's trunk wrinkled up into a frown. "I thought I saw you down by the Ndian river a few hours ago. Yes, that's right. You were gazing into your shell again and muttering about how perfectly-formed your beak was and how adorably slender you found your neck."

Tortoise wound his neck in a little bit and blinked two small, black eyes. "Oh no," he replied. "That wasn't me." He shuffled closer to Elephant and shook a crinkled foot at her. "You really should get those eyes tested, Ma Elephant. I was most certainly absolutely definitely NOT by the river last night." He adjusted his shell so that it shimmered in the sunlight and beside him Civet leapt from paw to paw.

"Conference! Conference! Conference! Conference! Conference!" he yelped.

Civet was the only animal in Korup who got excited by the actual conference, but then again Civet could get excited by anything, even mouldy eggs. He had tried to be a nocturnal, solitary animal like the rest of his kind, but the trouble was, he was far too hyperactive and needy to sit by while the other animals had all the fun. If something was happening, Civet *had* to be there.

Elephant dipped her trunk and then seconds later a noise began, a noise so low and rumbling it sounded as if it were coming from deep inside the mountain itself. But it wasn't coming from there, it was coming from Elephant's mouth – and high above the animals, from somewhere up in the clouds, another animal answered.

"Skreeeeeaghh!" A large bird burst out of the clouds and

wheeled above them, shredding the sky with each beat of its wings. Then it vanished amongst the clouds again.

"Show off," Hornbill muttered.

"Aunty!" Elephant bellowed. "We'd like to come up for our annual conference. Would you be so kind as to drop the ladder?"

A flash of brown-black feathers darted out from the clouds. "Coming your way now!" Ma Eagle cried.

Seconds later, something very long and very green tumbled down from the sky: it was a ladder made from the hanging vines in the forest, and it stretched from Mount Yuhan where the animals were standing, right up into the clouds.

Hornbill groaned, then put a wing over his eyes.

Leopard dipped her head towards him. "You could try flying up with your eyes closed."

Hornbill's beak widened as if Leopard had said something obscene. "FLYING UP WITH MY EYES CLOSED? Do you think I'm *mad*?"

Elephant wrapped her trunk around the sides of the ladder then placed an enormous foot on the first rung. And then, one by one, the animals followed, until just Tortoise remained on the mountain top.

He narrowed his beady eyes at the others then cleared his throat. "Ahem."

Civet glanced down, then jumped off the ladder, scooped Tortoise up onto his back, and began climbing – for he knew Tortoise's tiny feet wouldn't manage the wide gaps between the ladder rungs. But Tortoise didn't say thank you; the idea never even occurred to him. He simply nestled into Civet's fur, stretched out his neck as far as it would go and gazed lovingly at his reflection. And all the while Civet climbed rung after rung of the giant ladder.

Eventually, after a lot of huffing from Elephant, puffing from Leopard, grunting from Civet and grumbling from Hornbill, the animals arrived at the lowest-hanging cloud.

The top of the ladder was swallowed by mist and at the sight of it, Tortoise muttered, "About time, Pa Civet. You took a while on that climb, you know."

Before Elephant had a chance to berate Tortoise for his lack of manners, a feathered head poked out through the cloud. Eagle beckoned them on with a scaled talon. "This way."

There was a lot of bumping bottoms and elbows in eyes as the animals scrambled off the ladder into the cloud, but soon they emerged on top of it and even Hornbill found himself emitting a little cry of pleasure. Up above the clouds the sky was pure blue and it stretched out for miles. The animals (all except Hornbill who didn't want to antagonise his vertigo) peered over the edge of one cloud down to Korup below: at the ironwood, ebony and kola trees, now shrunk to the size of matchsticks, and at the Mana river, reduced to a wiggly thread.

Now, the type of people who love conferences might tell you that clouds are 'visible masses of condensed water vapour floating in the atmosphere' and that there is no way an elephant, a leopard, an African civet, a hornbill, a tortoise and a crowned eagle could have sat in one without falling right through. But those sorts of people often think rather dry, unimaginative thoughts like that. Wiser people would understand that clouds are not in fact water vapour at all. They are dreams stored up by crowned eagles and flown down to children's houses in the middle of the night. And dreams aren't watery and full of vapour – they are strong and wily, and they will hold your weight all right.

And so the animals settled into a particularly fleecy cloud and for a while none of them said anything at all. They simply sat and marvelled at the never-ending sky. Even Civet was silent for several minutes. Then Eagle flew from animal to animal taking names, because I'm afraid every conference, even one in the sky, begins with name taking. Elephant, Leopard, Hornbill and Civet gave their names but when Eagle came to Tortoise, the little creature tugged the bird's wing down low so that only she could hear and muttered: "My name is All-una."

Eagle frowned. "Really? I thought you were Pa Tortoise."

Tortoise stiffened. "I used to be called Tortoise but Ma Buffalo re-named me All-una, which means *Everybody* – because I spend so much of my time helping everybody else."

Although surprised, Eagle thought it best not to argue with the tortoise. After all, they were a long way up in the sky and falling out with each other would mean falling out of the cloud – and that was bound to end in tears.

When everybody was sitting comfortably, the conference began. The animals started by discussing whether they were all getting enough food and they agreed that they were, though Civet complained he hadn't caught many snakes in the rainforest recently (none of the other animals had the heart to tell him that it was because his hunting techniques – singing and dancing while approaching prey – were doomed). The animals discussed their health and shelters and apart from Hornbill (who had built his nest inside a hole in a tree which was repeatedly raided by chimpanzees hunting for eggs for their morning omelettes), the animals felt reasonably content with their arrangements.

Before long, the conference came to an end and it was time for food – a necessary part of the event because without it, Leopard might well have snapped up Hornbill or Eagle might have gobbled down Tortoise, and it is very hard to talk business when you're thinking of eating your colleague.

And so, in an unusual show of helpfulness, Tortoise volunteered to hold the ladder steady while Guenon (a monkey with particularly opposable thumbs, which meant he was often in charge of Carrying Important Things), climbed off the top rung cradling a large pot of food.

Tortoise smiled, the sort of smile that curls lips and darkens eyes. "So, who is this food for then, Pa Guenon?"

The monkey laid the pot down and wiped his brow. "For All-Una."

Tortoise beamed then he tugged the spoon out from under Guenon's arm and proceeded to shovel mouthful after mouthful of food from the pot into his greedy little beak.

Elephant started forward. "Where are your manners, Pa Tortoise? You know that no animal starts the conference lunch until everybody has been served a portion by Ma Eagle!"

Tortoise licked a dribble of food from his beak but instead of apologising, he simply shrugged. "Pa Guenon said the food was for All-Una and I think you'll find, Ma Elephant," he spooned another mouthful into his beak, "that I am he."

Leopard snarled. "You are Pa Tortoise and you're a greedy little monster!"

Tortoise chuckled. "Ask Ma Eagle if you don't believe me. She has the register."

Eagle's eyes narrowed as she scanned the list of names. "I have an All-Una but there is no mention of a Pa Tortoise at all."

Tortoise guzzled more and more food down until he was scraping the remains from the bottom of the pan. He let out a long, satisfied belch and then looked up at the other animals. "You see, my real name is actually All-Una and Pa Guenon did say that the food was for All-Una so it stands to reason that I should eat it *all*." He smirked at the animals and tried to ignore the fact that he had eaten so much food his body now felt incredibly snug and not altogether comfortable inside his shell.

Leopard snarled. "You are Pa Tortoise and we all know it!"

Eagle's feathers bristled and one by one the animals stepped closer to Tortoise and the empty pot of food.

"Liar!" they chorused. "Liar!"

Tortoise's smirk slipped from his face and, on seeing Leopard's teeth flashing in the sunlight, he tucked his head inside his shell. "I... I..." he stammered.

Leopard's stomach growled. Civet's mouth watered.

Tortoise squeaked. "Oh, Ma Leopard! Oh, Pa Civet! Please don't eat me!"

Elephant stamped her foot and the cloud beneath them trembled. "You have eaten ALL our food, Pa Tortoise, and you tricked Ma Eagle!"

Civet's eyes lit up and he leapt up and down. "Shall we eat Pa Tortoise?"

Tortoise retreated into his shell again.

Elephant shook his head. "No. There will be plenty of food for you all back down in the rainforest."

Despite his fear, Tortoise couldn't help but give a little snigger inside his shell. Then he stuck his head out and feigned a thankful look. "Oh thank you, Aunty."

But Elephant did not smile. "It's an awfully long way back down that ladder. Isn't it, Pa Tortoise?"

Tortoise nodded.

Leopard grinned, slowly understanding what Elephant was meaning. "Such a long way down…"

Hornbill's eyes widened as he, too, caught on. "Such a very long way down…"

Civet had no idea what anyone was talking about but was excited nonetheless. "Such a very, very long way down…"

Tortoise blinked. "And may I ask which of you kind animals will be carrying me on their back?"

There was a long silence, filled only by the wind rippling

through the clouds.

"Ma Elephant?" Tortoise asked. "You'll carry me, won't you?"

Without answering, Elephant dug her trunk into the cloud and trundled back down the ladder. Hornbill followed nervously, then Leopard, too, slinked from sight.

Tortoise shifted from one foot to the other then looked up at Civet. "Ah, Pa Civet, the kindest animal in Korup. Might I trouble you for a lift down?"

Civet cocked his head to one side and grinned. He knew he was meant to be cross about something but the whole conference had been so profoundly exciting he couldn't remember what he was meant to be cross about. But, scared of being left out, he disappeared beneath the cloud to join the other animals on their climb down to Mount Yuhan.

Tortoise stood alone on the cloud beside the empty pot, his heart hammering inside his shell.

"Well, it looks like you'll have to jump," came a voice from behind him.

Tortoise turned round to see Eagle perched on the cloud, her huge wings tucked proudly by her sides.

Tortoise bowed to her. "Majesty of the Sky, would you be so kind as to fly me down?"

Eagle pruned her feathers. "Fly you down? After you were late to the gathering in the first place? After you forgot to thank Pa Civet for carrying you up here? After you lied to me and ate all of the food?"

Tortoise blushed through his wrinkled skin. Put like that, it didn't sound good.

With a sharp cry, Eagle leapt from the cloud and disappeared into the dazzling blue sky.

Tortoise pushed through the cloud to the ladder. In the distance, far below him, he could still make out Civet. "Pa Civet!" he called. "At least tell my wife to lay out some leaves so that I have a soft landing when I jump."

Civet's reply spiralled up to Tortoise a few seconds later. "I'll have a word with her. Enjoy your jump! I'm extremely excited about watching it."

It was clear Civet now had absolutely no recollection of recent events. He hopped off the last rung of the ladder and bounced up to Elephant. "Pa Tortoise is going to leap from the clouds to the ground. It's going to be spectacular! I'll send word to his wife to lay out a bed of leaves for his landing, then we can all gather round and watch!" He bounced up and down, then chased his tail in a circle.

Elephant waited until Civet had calmed down and then she looked at him long and hard. "Think, Pa Civet. Why didn't we carry Pa Tortoise down the ladder?"

Civet panted into the mid-afternoon heat. "Um... Er... Because we forgot to?"

Leopard rolled her eyes.

And then Civet remembered. "Pa Tortoise ate our food!" he yapped.

Leopard nodded. "Exactly. Which is why we will tell Pa

Tortoise's wife exactly how he behaved today and then she can decide whether or not he deserves a bed of leaves for his landing – or something a little," she paused and chuckled to herself, "harder."

And so, while the animals went to find Ma Tortoise, Pa Tortoise himself waited on the top rung of the ladder. Night fell, and here and there, between the clouds, stars pricked the sky. Tortoise grumbled and muttered to himself and then, just as he was feeling well and truly fed up, he noticed movements down below. Animals had gathered around the foot of the ladder on Mount Yuhan and – Tortoise's heart leapt – they had arranged something for him to land on! He smiled to himself. His wife had brought the leaves – which was kind, actually, considering Tortoise had treated her rather badly over the years. He had never helped her cook the children supper, he had never bothered to offer a hand with the cleaning and he had most certainly never thought about trying to make their shelter better and safer.

Tortoise loosened his grip on the rung and then, with his breath held tight, leapt from the ladder. He hurtled through the air –

Down...

Down...

Down...

And as he fell he grinned smugly. He'd been late for the gathering on Mount Yuhan, he hadn't thanked Civet for the ride up into the clouds, he'd lied to Eagle and eaten all of the food – but he'd

got away with it all. He allowed himself a little glimpse into his shiny shell and his reflection beamed back at him.

Tortoise focused back on his descent and it was only then that he realised what his wife had really laid out on the ground. His stomach tightened, sweat clung to his skin and his beak dropped open.

His wife had not fetched a deliciously soft bed of leaves for him. Oh no. She had laid out a pile of ROCKS!

Tortoise back-pedalled with two feet and flapped with the others but nothing could stop his descent. Preparing for the worst, he tucked his body inside his precious shell, begged for forgiveness in a terrified little croak, and crashed down onto the pile of rocks.

Hornbill fainted immediately, but the rest of the animals surrounding the rocks were absolutely still, watching. And then, very slowly, Tortoise poked his head out of his shell.

"Am – am I alive?" he croaked.

Civet sniffed him. "Yes, but your shell is a bit wonky."

Tortoise extended his neck and curled it round but his shell did not cast back his reflection. Instead Tortoise found himself looking at a distorted jumble of bumps and lumps and scratches and dips. He gasped.

"No! Not my shell!"

Elephant smiled. "Now perhaps that will be a lesson to you, Pa Tortoise, that you should spend less time looking at yourself in your shell and more time looking outwards at those around you."

Tortoise kicked a rock.

"You must try to be punctual when animals are waiting on you," Elephant went on. "You must thank those who help you, you must tell the truth at all times and you must share before taking for yourself." She paused. "Above all, Pa Tortoise, you must be kind."

Tortoise huffed and Civet frowned. "What did he do wrong again?"

But Elephant only sighed. Then she set off down the mountain with the other animals until only Tortoise was left on the top of Mount Yuhan. He looked around at the Korup region, at the way the land rose and dipped like the backs of sleeping giants and the way the Ndian river curled through the rainforest in near soundless murmurs. But Tortoise could find no comfort in his beautiful surroundings or in the wisdom of Elephant's words. His pride was dented. So was his shell. And with a grunt, he trundled back down the mountain.

Why the Dog and the Drill Monkey are Enemies

Adèle Geras

The dog and the drill monkey are sworn enemies. Everyone knows that. The dogs hunt the drills and the drills snarl and cry and run away from the dogs. They fight. They always fight. The drills have grown terrified of the very smell of the dogs who spend their days chasing them.

Long ago, things were very different in the jungle. Then Man came, a two-legged animal who cut and slashed his way through the territory which had always belonged to creatures with four legs, or two claws, or those who had no legs at all and slipped through the leaves like water moving over the river bed.

In those days, long ago, the trees and creepers of the jungle spread from beyond the mountain where the sun rose to the river bank where every evening you could see it setting, sinking into the water like a round stone made of fire. The creatures of the jungle filled the branches of the ironwood trees, and sheltered under the leaves of the umbrella trees. They climbed the strangler vines and filled the dim spaces under the ebony trees with their sounds: chirping, squawking, rustling, crying, screeching. It was never silent in the jungle. The animals and birds who lived there wandered through the green, looking for food, and every kind of creature found a shelter and a home in the jungle's trees and roots and creepers.

The seasons changed. The rains came and the green became greener as the leaves on every tree uncurled from their buds, and the crops sprang out of the soil. The Akpasang and Mana rivers burst their banks and the rain made so much noise when it fell that the creatures stopped their chattering and chittering and chirping and took cover where they could.

The drill monkeys lived in one of the tallest trees. Pa Drill was leader of the tribe. He was married to Ma Drill and had many children, the oldest of whom was called Prince Drill because he was handsome and proud and ran through the jungle accompanied by his friends, who whooped and shrieked and tore the creepers from the trees as they swung about, playing games and making mischief.

"Your eldest son throws nuts down on us when we're curled up sleeping," said the pangolin.

"Prince Drill finds me where I'm sleeping," said the green tree snake, "and pulls my tail. Then he runs away before I can unwind and bite him."

"Your son," said the great blue turaco to Ma Drill, "is too wild. Everyone in the jungle is growing tired of his tricks. He steals food from us. He comes up behind us and makes a loud noise and startles us. His best friend is Brown Dog, youngest son of the Dog family who live with Man, and together, they terrify every creature they meet who happens to be smaller and weaker. Can't you speak to him?"

Ma Drill sighed. She was sitting on the river bank and Ma

Turaco was perched on a nearby branch. "What you are telling me is true, Aunty. But I don't know what to do with him," she confessed. "He's always been hard to manage. My other children are as good as gold but Prince has always been....well, a little wild. But it's my opinion that Brown Dog is to blame for much of the wildness. There is no controlling Brown Dog at all."

"I will have a word with Brown Dog's father," said Ma Turaco. And she flew out of the trees and went to where the dogs had their encampment close to the edge of Man's village.

"Good morning, Uncle," said Ma Turaco, settling herself on a rock. The dog tribe were all there, lying around, sleeping in the sunshine. It was too hot to hunt until the sun moved a little lower in the sky.

"Where is your son, Brown Dog?" Ma Turaco asked.

"I don't know," said Pa Dog. "I never know where he is. He and Prince Drill are too much for me to manage. They are great friends and no one in the jungle is safe when they're on the rampage."

Ma Turaco nodded her head and the blue feathers on her crest trembled in the light breeze. "I have an idea. I think Brown Dog should find himself a wife. If he had to provide for his children and look after his family, he'd have less time for idle mischief. When their young arrive, most creatures calm down a little. Brown Dog's main duty will be hunting for food for his pups."

Ma Dog, who had been listening to this conversation, sniffed the morning air and sat up a little straighter. "A wedding! Yes, Ma Turaco, I think that is a very good idea. I will enjoy arranging it. We'll ask all our friends."

The whole of the Dog family discussed the matter of Brown Dog's wedding at the evening meal.

"It will be a splendid occasion," said Ma Dog. "I will prepare the tastiest feast anyone in the jungle has ever eaten."

"I can invite all my friends," said Brown Dog's sister. "All the birds and the porcupines and the pangolins and the duikers…."

"And the Drills," said Brown Dog. "Prince Drill is my best friend so he must stand beside me at my wedding."

"Yes, the Drills, of course. And the tribes of dogs and drills from other parts of the jungle," said Pa Dog.

The whole dog clan discussed the wedding, backwards and forwards, yapping and barking.

Brown Dog fell silent. He began to gnaw at a bone lying on the ground, and looked up at his mother.

"Why aren't you saying anything?" asked Ma Dog.

"You're all busy arranging my wedding without asking if there's anyone I would like to marry. Or if I'm ready to settle down."

Pa Dog looked stern. "As head of this tribe, I am telling you and not asking you, my son. It'll do you good to be married. A family of your own will calm you down. Your mother and I are tired of making excuses about your wild behaviour. If you haven't decided which of the beautiful young dogs you'd like to settle down with, I will give you some time to meet them and choose the one you like best."

So Brown Dog stopped running around and making mischief and turned his attention to finding someone to settle down with. He went first to a pretty dog sitting under the kola tree. She was the oldest and most respected of all the young lady dogs.

"Would you like to live with me? My ma says it's time for me to settle down. I am asking you to marry me."

The dog didn't answer for a while but continued grooming her splendid tail.

"Please?" Brown Dog asked again.

Finally she said, "I would rather live in an anthill, Brown Dog. There would be no peace if I lived with you. You are noisy and wild and I like a quiet life."

"But if I marry you," said Brown Dog, "you will calm me down and make me much quieter. I would probably be almost silent. My ma and pa say that marriage would be good for me."

"Good for you perhaps," she said. "But not good for me. Bye bye, Brown Dog. Look somewhere else."

Brown Dog went from one young female to another and every one of them said, "No, Brown Dog, I do not want to marry you. Find someone else." He was too wild, they said. Too noisy. Too difficult to live with.

In the end, he came to White Flower, who was the youngest of his cousins from the Falls area.

"You are prettier than all the other dogs I've met," said Brown Dog. "I don't suppose you'd like to marry me, would you?"

"I would love to marry you," said White Flower.

"You don't think I'm too wild? Too noisy?" Brown Dog asked, astonished.

"Not at all. I think you're daring and exciting. I love hearing stories of your adventures. I laugh when I hear about the things you've done."

"Oh, thank you, dear White Flower!" said Brown Dog. "I am going to tell my ma at once. She will be so delighted."

Ma Dog was thrilled. "You've never mentioned her," she said. "It's true that a white dog is quite rare in these parts. Is she pretty? Does she like you?"

"She does," Brown Dog smiled. "And she is very pretty indeed."

"I will go to the Falls area tomorrow, then," said Pa Dog "and speak to our cousins, Small Ma and Small Pa, White Flower's parents."

So, it was decided. Brown Dog was to marry White Flower, the beautiful young dog who lived near the Falls. Ma Dog started preparing the feast, sending every bird she knew to the furthest parts of the jungle to find the best foods. And Brown Dog asked Prince Drill to the feast, and to stand beside him at the wedding.

"But before the wedding," he said, "I would like you to meet White Flower. And I would like her to meet you. Her parents, Small Ma and Small Pa, are coming to visit us and my mother has invited some very close friends to a meal. It won't be quite as splendid as the Wedding Feast, but I would like you to come and see my beautiful bride."

"Nothing I'd like better," said Prince Drill, smiling at his friend. "Everyone I meet tells me how wonderful she is, how pretty and how kind. I am very eager to meet her."

So it was decided. Prince Drill and his mother and father, Ma Drill and Pa Drill were to eat with the Dog tribe and meet White Flower. Brown Dog was happy, and why shouldn't he be? His best friend was about to meet the young lady dog he was preparing to marry.

"There's just one thing I ought to mention," said Brown Dog. "Please eat as tidily as you can. My Ma doesn't want any bones thrown on the floor. If you do such a thing, I won't be able to control myself and I'll jump down from the table and start gnawing them. I can't help myself. I am, after all, a hunting dog."

"But I don't see the problem," Prince Drill said. "Isn't White Flower a dog too? Wouldn't she join you on the floor, gnawing at the bone?"

"Oh no!" Brown Dog looked horrified. "White Flower is the most refined dog I have ever met. Even though she admires me and thinks my adventures are amusing, she herself is very well-behaved. In fact," his voice dropped and he whispered in Prince Drill's ear, "Small Pa and Small Ma aren't too happy about the wedding. They think we hunting dogs are…a little rough. Vulgar. Uncouth. I want to impress her, my friend, and show her that she's marrying someone who knows how to be polite and genteel."

"Very well," said Prince Drill. "I will do as you ask."

When Prince Drill met White Flower, something terrible happened. Brown Dog was sure that his friend and his wife-to-be would like one another at once, but the very opposite was true.

"It's good to meet you," said Prince Drill when he was introduced, but he was thinking: *She looks very stuck up to me and not nearly as pretty as Brown Dog said she was. I don't like her one bit. She's already acting as if she is the most important person in Brown Dog's life.*

"How do you do?" said White Flower, putting out her nose so that Prince Drill could touch it with his own. This was the way dogs greeted one another and Prince Drill was a little surprised to be asked to behave in such an unmonkey-like manner. "I'm delighted to meet you, too." What she was thinking was: *He's* vulgar and has no manners. Once I'm married, I will see to it that my mate has as little to do with Prince Drill as possible. He will not be a good influence on any children. I don't think much of any of the Drills, but I will make sure that Brown Dog doesn't go about quite so much with his smelly friend.

The feast began at sunset. Ma Dog had prepared meat for the dogs and fruits and nuts for the monkeys and everyone agreed it was a most delicious meal. But Prince Drill was getting angrier and angrier. Brown Dog had eyes for no one but White Flower and didn't speak to his old friend at all.

He asked me not to throw bones on the ground, but he's so taken up with his wife-to-be that he won't notice, I'm sure. I'll test him...let's see if his love is stronger than his nature.

And as the stars glittered in the dark sky and the full moon lit up the clearing where the feast was being held, Prince Drill picked a bone up from the table. He glanced over to where Brown Dog was sitting and yes, his friend was still nuzzling White Flower and not even bothering to eat.

Ha! thought Prince Drill. *Let's see what happens if I just...*

He threw a handful of bones down on the earth next to where Brown Dog was sitting and before anyone knew what was happening, Brown Dog had jumped down from the table and begun chewing on the bones, making hoarse growling noises in his throat.

"Oh!" cried Small Ma. "What do you think you're doing, Brown Dog? Ugh, what dreadful behaviour. How wild! How rude!"

Brown Dog didn't answer. He was too busy cracking the bones between his teeth.

"How unseemly! How undignified! How brutal and dog-like!" said Small Pa.

"We can't let our beautiful White Flower marry such a creature," said Small Ma. "Come, White Flower, come with us. We are going back to the Falls. Say thank you to Pa and Ma Dog for their hospitality."

"Stop! Please stop!" Ma Dog shrieked. "I'm sure we can come to some arrangement…please! I so wanted to prepare a wedding." She started to howl.

"I'm very sorry," said Small Ma. "We can't consider a marriage between your son and our daughter. It's quite clear

that he's never going to change his ways. It's in his nature to be wild and rude."

And off they went, into the dark spaces between the bush mango trees, with White Flower following ruefully behind them.

Brown Dog, who had finished gnawing at the bones, was now angry with Prince Drill, angrier than he'd ever been in his life. "I warned him," he said to his parents. "I told him that I wouldn't be able to stop myself from eating what was thrown from the table... He promised me he wouldn't. He's a false, false friend."

He turned to Prince Drill. "I'm too full of food to chase you now, but tomorrow will be a different story altogether and then take care. I will come after you. I will hound you through trees and creepers from dawn to dusk. You will have no mercy from me, nor from any of my tribe. Forever."

So that is how things stand now. The dogs hunt the drill monkeys and the drills hate the dogs who hunt them. But once, a long time ago, they were friends. And that is the end of the story.

Why it is Believed Tortoises Live Forever

Ifeoma Onyefulu

One very hot afternoon, Pa Leopard, the king, called an urgent meeting. The temperature on that particular day – had anyone bothered to check – was as hot as the Sahara Desert in the middle of the afternoon! No wonder it felt as if a giant hand had been placed on top of the heads of the animals. Despite the extreme heat, the jungle creatures dropped everything and hurried to Leopard's palace. Mind you, it was the fifth meeting Leopard had called in a week!

Leopard had purposely built his beautiful palace on the Namata ledges, high above the forest, and from there he could see much of the jungle. He could see ironwood trees, which are as strong as bricks, umbrella trees, loved by birds and monkeys alike, and of course the bush mango trees. Also, from his palace he could see Mount Yuhan, the tallest mountain, and some of the smaller hills and valleys below. Indeed, a breath-taking sight!

It did not take long for most of the animals to arrive. The last animal to arrive was Pa Tortoise, which wasn't at all surprising for he was a thinker. He was always thinking of ways he could impress everyone. No wonder it took him ages to get anywhere.

When Tortoise arrived at the palace, his friend Ma Buffalo had saved him a seat in the back row where they both liked to sit.

Tortoise turned to his friend. "What's the meeting about?" he asked, hoping it was not another competition as he needed more time for thinking. Buffalo said that she didn't know, after all the meeting had just started.

Leopard thanked everyone for coming, and then – like a politician – launched into his favourite phrase. It was the same phrase he had used at the last meeting. "An active body is an active mind," he said loudly.

Tortoise groaned. He knew instantly that Leopard was planning another competition. "When am I ever going to have the time to think?" he muttered to himself, miserably.

"I have some great news," Leopard announced, his fur shining brightly with excitement. And straight away the ears of the animals shot up like stones fired from several catapults. "Everyone will love this," Leopard added enthusiastically. "I am organising a dancing competition. And everyone is going to have lots of fun, trust me!"

Tortoise's head was spinning round and round like a wheel. In fact, he nearly passed out with shock because dancing was not his favourite pastime. What's more, the last competition had been a nightmare; it had been a singing competition. Poor Tortoise had lost his voice when it was his turn to sing and not a sound had come out of his parched throat! It had been awful.

However, on the day of the dancing competition, all the animals, including Tortoise, danced.

Again, his performance wasn't something you'd want to tell your grandchildren about, and he knew it.

So, he began to think what he could do to really impress everyone. Well, he could try boasting. Everyone knew he was very good at that! He could impress the animals by telling them all the things he could do. So he vowed to give it a try.

Several weeks later, Leopard organised another event, and this time it was a cooking competition. Lots of animals were excited about it, but not Tortoise. He didn't know how to cook and came last in the competition. Still, he saw a chance to boast to his friend, Buffalo.

"I could have won that competition, you know," he said, "but I was kind enough to let someone else win."

Buffalo smiled politely.

Encouraged by this, Tortoise thought, *I must boast some more! I will tell my friend I can do incredible things, and then one day everyone will sit up and take notice of me.* But he could not think of a single incredible thing to say.

For the next competition, Leopard organised an eating competition. Tortoise immediately paid Buffalo a visit at her house, and they talked about the skills and strategies required for as challenging a competition as shovelling food into one's mouth.

Soon Tortoise began boasting again. He told Buffalo, "I'm going to win. This competition is too easy, you'll see."

Finally, Buffalo couldn't keep Tortoise's boastings to herself any longer, and as soon as her friend had left, she rushed off to spread *nkongassa* amongst the other animals. Oh, how they laughed at the gossip! No one took Tortoise very seriously after that.

Days went by and Tortoise carried on boasting. Then one day, Buffalo snapped.

"Look, my friend," she said to Tortoise, "there is nothing you can say or do that will impress me anymore. Why, you can't even beat a kitten in an arm wrestling competition!"

Tortoise was completely astonished. He had thought all his boastings had impressed Buffalo! What more could he do?

"You wait and see! I am very strong. I can even win a game of tug-of-war against two elephants both pulling at the same time," he said confidently.

Buffalo almost fell off her chair with shock. "Don't make me laugh, Pa Tortoise!" she said. "How can you possibly defeat two elephants, eh?"

But Tortoise persisted. "I promise you I can win a game of tug-of-war against two elephants."

Buffalo stared at him. *Is my friend feeling all right? Has he got a fever or something?* she wondered.

Tortoise smiled broadly. "By this time tomorrow, I will show you two elephants who will testify that I beat them at a tug-of-war," he said, as confidently as a warrior. "My only request is that you don't ask me how I won the game, ok?"

Buffalo had no choice but to agree.

The two friends placed a bet. If Tortoise won the game, his

friend would pay him, and if he lost, he would pay Buffalo.

So, the following day, Tortoise set out to find two elephants willing to play the game with him. He went all the way down a very steep valley to the river, a favourite place for the elephants. They usually went there for their early morning swim and a splash about in the water for their little ones. But on that day, the river was empty.

"Where are all the elephants when I need them?" Tortoise muttered anxiously to himself as he crawled back up the steep valley. He had a right to be anxious. If he failed to find any elephants, his friend would certainly laugh at him, or worse, he could lose his friend altogether. Where indeed were the elephants?

The sun, by now, was shining brightly; soon everywhere would be as hot as an oven. But Tortoise had a task at hand, and nothing was going to stop him. So, he decided he would go to the home of the elephants. Surely, that is where he would find them!

The elephants' home was quite far away, and it took Tortoise a while to get there. Oddly enough, he did not mind. You see, the distance gave him an opportunity to think. He needed to work out how he was going to persuade two elephants to take part in a tug-of-war game!

But sadly for him, when he got there, the elephants had already left. Oh, you can imagine how distressed he was! He wished he had some magic powers that would show him where the elephants were. Worse still, as he turned a corner, there was Buffalo.

"Have you found any elephants yet?" Buffalo asked, and he said no. "Look, my friend," began Buffalo, "you must not make promises you can't keep, because you can get into lots of trouble," she warned him.

Nevertheless, Tortoise set off once again, wondering where he was going to go next. He had no plans at all; his mind was as empty as a banana leaf. Was all that bragging finally catching up with him?

Suddenly, he felt the ground shake. It was as if some huge animal were jumping up and down. Tortoise moved quickly, eager to find out what was going on. Seconds later, he saw an adult elephant exercising at a distance. No wonder the ground was shaking so much! Tortoise was very happy to see him.

The elephant was so busy jogging on the spot that he didn't see Tortoise watching him. "One, two, three…!" the elephant said, counting the seconds as he jogged. He was determined to lose some weight.

Tortoise hesitated for a second. *How on earth am I going to persuade this elephant to take part in a tug-of-war game with me?* he wondered.

He cleared his throat and said to the jogging elephant, "I am little, but I can beat you in a game of tug-of-war if the rope is so long that you can't see the other end."

The elephant stopped jogging for a moment and looked down. "I beg your pardon. What did you say?"

Tortoise cleared his throat once more. "I am little, but I can beat you in a game of tug-of-war if the rope is so long that you can't see the other end," he said.

The elephant was now fuming like a kerosene stove. "How ridiculous is this little fella! Oh, what an insult!" he muttered darkly. Then he added to himself: *How can he even think of asking me to compete in a tug-of-war game?*

Nevertheless, he finally said yes to Tortoise, and let him know that he did not care how long the rope was. But, out of curiosity, he said, "If I can't see the rope, how can I be sure you won't tie one end to a very big tree?" He knew how smart Tortoise was.

"What? Don't you trust me?" Tortoise replied, pretending to be upset by what the elephant had just said. "You mustn't worry because you're going to feel an equal pull on the other end."

"Equal pull?" the elephant spat out in disgust. He was very annoyed by what he had just heard.

Before the elephant could walk away, Tortoise quickly set a time and place for the tug-of-war game. Then he beat a hasty retreat.

Now that he had found one elephant, Tortoise had to find the second one. He set off in the opposite direction. By now, the sun had hidden behind a cloud, and Tortoise feared it would rain before the event could start.

Soon, he saw a second elephant shadow boxing under a tree. He was concentrating so hard on punching the air, he did not notice Tortoise.

"Hello, Uncle," said Tortoise cheerfully.

Elephant number two stopped for a moment. "Hello," he replied coldly. He did not like anyone interrupting his workout. Nevertheless, Tortoise quickly repeated the words he had said to the first elephant.

The second elephant was horrified. "What, a tug-of-war with you?" he asked in disbelief. He was very sceptical; he couldn't imagine playing such a game with an animal that small!

Eventually, Tortoise was able to persuade him to take part as well. He gave the elephant a different location, but the time of the event remained the same. Then he hurried off.

When Tortoise was out of sight, he tied together many strong liana cords to form one very long rope. He gave one end of the rope to the first elephant, and asked him to wait until he felt a slight tug on it before starting to pull. Tortoise now rushed over to the second elephant, gave him the other end of the rope and repeated the same instructions. All this rushing around was exhausting for Tortoise but it was worth it.

Finally, he went to the centre of the rope and gave it a good tug. Then he stood back. The two elephants, feeling the tug on the rope, began pulling as strongly as they could, without knowing that Tortoise was not on the other end of it.

They pulled and pulled the rope with all their might, determined to never, ever lose to a small animal like Tortoise! After a few minutes, the poor elephants had no strength left and felt very dizzy indeed. Eventually, they collapsed on the ground like empty sacks of rice. Tortoise now rushed off to get Buffalo to tell her the great news!

"Ma Buffalo, my friend, you must come at once!" he

screamed all the way to Buffalo's front door. Buffalo, in a state of panic, dropped what she was doing and rushed out at once, and together they ran to where each elephant was still lying on the ground, exhausted.

Buffalo asked each of the elephants in turn, "Is it true that you were in a tug-of-war against Tortoise?" Both answered yes, and declared Tortoise the winner of the tug-of-war game.

Buffalo was very impressed. She said that any tortoise that strong deserved to live forever. Straight away she began spreading *nkongassa* about her friend. "Tortoise is so powerful, and he will live forever!" she told the animals.

This time, you will agree, the gossip was good! And Ma Buffalo was so good at spreading *nkongassa* that the entire jungle soon heard about Tortoise.

That is why, even today, it is believed that tortoises live forever.

Why the Hornbill Calls after Monkeys

Sarah Lean

A troop of guenon monkeys gathered at the top of the Namata ledge in the forest. They were well fed with kola nuts and looking for some fun. Excited chatter rose as they made plans to hold a monkey carnival. They whooped and screeched with excitement as it was announced that the carnival would end with a competition to see who had the longest tail.

Eager to find something eye-catching to add to their carnival costumes, the monkeys sprung from the rocks and leaped through the canopy in search of colourful feathers. The more feathers they added to their fur, the better dressed they would appear.

Meanwhile, the rainbow-coloured birds of the forest were snacking contentedly in the umbrella trees. Unaware of the naughty monkeys' intentions, the birds flapped into the air with fright as the monkeys pounced out from behind the dense leaves, leaping to pluck their feathers.

Soon, a message to keep away from the naughty monkeys passed between the birds, all except one. Pa Hornbill had a huge, curved and dangerous beak, and none of the monkeys dared to bother him.

But not everyone had found something dazzling to wear. Guenon, a small white-nosed monkey, hadn't yet snatched any feathers, but he was desperate to join the carnival and parade with the others. He hid in the canopy, gazing at the magnificent sleek, black tail feathers of the hornbill.

A last loose feather drifted down to the forest floor where a drill monkey was licking salt from the dried edge of a spring. Pa Drill caught the feather and sat down on his stumpy tail. He turned his serious face up, spotting the hornbill sitting there. Hornbill was preening his glossy wings with his long curved beak, humming softly to himself about how happy and proud he was of his long, sleek tail.

"Is this yours, Uncle?" the drill monkey called up through the trees, holding up the pink downy feather for the hornbill to see.

Hornbill huffed and turned away, irritated that the drill monkey had thought that such a tiny bit of fluff might belong to him.

"There's going to be a monkey carnival tomorrow morning," Drill continued, spotting the tip of Guenon's white nose poking through the leaves.

Hornbill didn't reply, busy with tending to his fine feathers.

Drill scratched at the salt. "Have you ever seen the carnival?" he asked, in case the hornbill didn't know what the naughty white-nosed monkey might be up to. "The monkeys steal feathers for their costumes."

Hornbill shrugged and quivered, fizzing from the tufts on

his head, right down to the tip of his long, black tail. Annoyed at being interrupted while preening, he turned a bright, dark eye on the drill monkey.

"Monkeys are not very clever," he said. "But most of them are smart enough to notice that I have no small pink feathers." Still peeved at the drill, he added, "And also smart enough to notice that I have a long and dangerous beak. They wouldn't dare try to take a feather from me."

From behind a branch, Guenon's small ears wriggled and his dull, speckled coat bristled. He was, like all the monkeys, smart enough to stay away from the bird with the long, dangerous beak. But he so wanted the glossy feathers of the hornbill to wear at the carnival and was prepared to wait quietly, listening, while he hatched a plan.

Pa Drill hadn't meant to offend the proud bird. "They're having a competition too," he said, so that the bird might know that he was only trying to be helpful. "To see who has the longest tail."

Hornbill turned his back so that the drill could see the whole of his long, magnificent tail.

"None of their tails are as long as mine," said the bird. "Perhaps I should enter. What's the prize for the longest tail?"

"The prize?" Drill said. He thought for a moment, but he hadn't heard a prize mentioned in all the monkey-chatter about the carnival. "The prize is that everyone will know who has the longest tail," he said, simply.

"That would be me," said Hornbill, laughing snootily.

Guenon was listening intently to the puffed-up hornbill. His bright orange eyes ran down the length of the hornbill's tail, and he so wanted to be able to say that the tail feathers belonged to him.

Quickly, Guenon sprang over to the rest of the troop and whispered in a monkey's ear. And, like typical monkeys, a rumour spread. Soon a name was chattered and scattered amongst them. Guenon returned to the canopy above the hornbill and the drill.

So far, Drill had not enjoyed the conversation with the rude hornbill, but when he heard the rumour spreading through Korup, he thought he should tell the bird what he heard.

"They're saying that Ma Mangabey has the longest tail in Korup," he said.

"Impossible!" said Hornbill.

Seeing that the hornbill was too full of himself and not prepared to listen, Drill turned his rainbow rump to him and walked quietly away.

Hornbill frowned, annoyed at what the drill had said. Surely everyone knew that the hornbill had the longest tail. He flitted through the trees, eager to find Ma Mangabey, the red-capped monkey with the so-called longest tail, while the little white-nosed monkey followed at a careful distance.

The monkeys were preparing for the carnival competition. One tucked small scarlet feathers behind his ears, dabbed red earth on his nose and painted his tail to match. Another fussed over a tiara of stolen silvery feathers around her head, and one waxed his moustache into curls, fluffing his beard and throat-ruff with the addition of some green feathers. Another slicked up some short black feathers on his head. All of their tails were long, but not as long or as sleek and beautiful as Hornbill's.

Ma Mangabey was tall and beautiful, and sat away from the others on the ground. She painted her eyelids with white clay. Her cheeks were fluffed with the addition of downy white feathers. Her lovely long tail arched all the way over her back and right over her head.

Pa Hornbill frowned at Ma Mangabey so hard that wrinkles circled his eyes. His neck shrunk into his shoulders at the thought of her winning the longest tail competition. He looked at his own tail, then at Mangabey's again. It was hard to tell which was the longest, but her tail was thin, with a silly white tuft on the end.

Having closely watched the proud hornbill, the patient little white-nosed monkey waited for exactly the right moment. He came out from where he had been hiding, although he still kept a sensible distance from the large, dangerous beak.

"That's a nice tail you've got," Guenon said casually, picking at nits on his hind leg. "Very long indeed."

Hornbill couldn't help fluffing up at the compliment, eyeing the speckled monkey with his short tail. He spread his wings to conceal the view of Mangabey below.

"The longest in Korup," Hornbill said, grinning from the long curve of his hard beak.

"Definitely," Guenon said, half turned away, as if there was nothing more important than the seeds that he chewed and spat out. Hornbill immediately liked the drab little monkey.

"You have a good eye," the hornbill smirked.

The little white-nosed monkey and the hornbill chatted politely for a minute and soon were talking about the carnival.

"Have you heard that Pa Colobus is going to win the carnival competition?" said Guenon.

"The red colobus monkey?" Hornbill said, flapping to regain his balance on the branch. "But you already said that I have the longest tail in Korup."

"You do have the longest tail," said Guenon, and moved away a little as the hornbill's long beak swung closer to him. "But the competition is for the most beautiful matching costume."

Hornbill glowered from the wrinkled circles of his eyes, cross that Pa Drill had deceived him.

"Matching?" he huffed.

Guenon picked seeds from his teeth and shrugged.

"The winner will be the one whose tail matches the rest of their outfit." He scratched his rump, pretending that the carnival competition didn't matter to him. "That's why Pa Colobus will win. He has red hair on his head, a red back *and* a red tail."

Hornbill scrunched his head into his neck. Pa Drill was obviously jealous and had been trying to fool him all along! It seemed obvious, however, that the little white-nosed monkey had no chance of winning the competition, as his tail was short and didn't match the rest of him, and Hornbill felt he had nothing to lose from finding out what Guenon knew.

"Can anyone enter the competition?" Hornbill said.

"Anyone who's brave enough."

Hornbill fluffed up again. His dangerous beak made him braver than all the other birds that had flown away, but it was a little too close to the white-nosed monkey for comfort.

Guenon swung away and was now hanging from one arm, reaching for a kola nut, as Hornbill turned around, looking at his matching wings and tail.

"All my feathers match too." Hornbill twirled on the branch. He could still win the competition.

Guenon secretly smiled at the hornbill's words. Pa Hornbill was falling for his trick.

"I can't see from here," Guenon said. "I want to get that particularly nice-looking kola nut over there, then I'll come back and have a good look." He swung and swung, reaching for the nut with his fingertips, taking his time. He squatted on a branch with the nut he had grasped.

"Well?" said Hornbill, scowling and becoming impatient. "A fine, competition-winning outfit, don't you think?"

"It's nice," Guenon said, glancing over, sinking his teeth into the nut.

"Nice? My very long, sleek and shiny, blackly-black tail is not only the longest, but look how it matches my wings and my back, and my neck and chest," Hornbill said, spinning on the spot. "*All* matching."

Guenon smiled. "It's a shame that it doesn't match your head though."

The wrinkles around Hornbill's eyes deepened.

"My head? But it's blackly-black and sleek and shiny too. Completely co-ordinated with the rest of me."

"But you're a white-crested hornbill…" Guenon raised his eyebrows. "Oh, of course, you can't see your own head."

Hornbill's eyes rolled around as he tried to see what it was impossible to see. He closed one eye, then the other, but all he could see was his long, horny beak.

"Please tell me my head is the deepest shiniest blackest sleekest shade of black too!" Hornbill moaned.

"Your head is pale and fluffy," said the little white-nosed monkey, as if he was very sorry for the bird.

"Pale?" Hornbill nearly fell off his perch, grunting and flapping to regain his balance. "And fluffy!"

"Whitish, I'd say," said Guenon.

Hornbill sagged into his shoulders.

"Don't worry," Guenon said, swinging closer to the bird. "All you need is something to match your head and then you will win."

"Like what?" groaned Hornbill.

Guenon looked around, pretending to search for something that fitted the bill, casually coming across his own short tail.

"You can have my tail if you want," Guenon said, popping the nut into his cheek pouch, and waving his fluffy-tipped white tail at the exasperated bird. "I don't mind swapping with yours."

"Is my head really fluffy and pale like your tail?"

With two nimble swings, Guenon landed beside Hornbill, now unafraid of the curved beak. He swept his tail across Hornbill's eyes like a feather boa.

"Exactly the same," said Guenon.

"Would I be completely matching if I had it?" Hornbill said, blinded by the whitish feathery tail, imagining how a paler head and tail would contrast beautifully with all his other dark feathers in the middle. Smart as a dinner jacket and shirt.

"It's yours if you want it," Guenon said. "I wouldn't stand a chance in the competition with it, but you…"

"I'm not sure," Hornbill said, hesitating, thinking how dull the monkey's tail was. "I'm very attached to my own tail. I've been flying with it since I was fledged and I'd probably miss it."

Guenon was still very close to that dangerous beak, but those long tail feathers were within his reach too.

"It's only a competition," he said, holding his nerve.

"Only a competition?" said Hornbill. This dull little monkey had no idea how it would feel to be called the most beautifully dressed in the whole of Korup. "Give me that tail of yours!"

Tails swapped, Guenon squeezed his lips around the nut, so he didn't grin too much.

"Just for the carnival," Hornbill said. "But you must give me my tail back straight afterwards."

"Just for the carnival," Guenon said, bouncing away through the forest. "Oh, I forgot to tell you," he called, "the carnival starts at noon."

"But the drill said it starts in the morning," Hornbill called back, flapping to keep his balance, feeling a little uncoordinated with the new tail. Why had he ever listened to that naughty drill monkey?

"But you don't want to come too early," Guenon said, from far away now. "Arrive fashionably late, and make an entrance." And he joined the rest of the troop who were busy grooming their tails.

Hornbill spent the next morning fluffing up his new tail

and smoothing out his wings, imagining exactly how fine he must look. This was a big day for the bird, who was desperate to show off his new matching tail, and although he didn't like to fly unless he had to, he headed for the clearing where the canopy opened up to the sky.

But there was no troop of monkeys where the carnival was to be held, only some small tatty, balding birds drooped on the branches. There was no sound of excitement or alarm, or any monkeys greeting, parading or competing at all. Surely there should be monkeys finishing off their furry makeup, finding last minute feathers for their outfits!

"I'm here for the competition!" Hornbill called, a little flustered. "I'm ready. Is anyone going to challenge me for the most beautiful matching outfit?"

There was no carnival to be seen. No parade, no monkeys, and no competition. Hornbill began to feel foolish, swaying on the branch to stay upright.

A voice rose from the forest floor.

"Poor Pa Hornbill," Drill said. "Did those naughty monkeys trick you?"

Hornbill was practically spitting feathers, and he cawed noisily. How could someone with such a long, dangerous beak be tricked by a small monkey? He turned around and looked at the tail he now wore, grunting and screeching, infuriated at Guenon.

"I did try to warn you," Drill said. "The poor birds of Korup are almost bald and now you have lost your tail completely."

Hornbill screeched again. "Where is Guenon?"

"I think the troop went that-a-way," Drill said, pointing into the deepest part of the forest. "But if I were you, I'd fly in the opposite direction in case they trick your wings away from you too."

"I want my tail back!" Hornbill squawked. Once again, taking no notice of Drill, he flew off unsteadily to find the white-nosed monkey.

From amongst the pea green shades of the forest, the sound of the white-nosed monkey's triumph reached Hornbill's ears.

"Look at me! Look at my tail," Guenon sang happily to himself, preening his fine, new, long tail.

As the shadow of the angry hornbill circled above them, the monkeys spread the word that the bird with the dangerous beak was coming.

Hornbill shrieked from the sky. He dived into the canopy and landed heavily and shakily on a nearby branch as the monkeys swiftly leaped out of his way.

"The carnival is over. Give me back my tail!" he squawked at Guenon.

"It's mine now," Guenon said, hopping away and mingling with the other monkeys. "I won the competition for the longest tail."

Fuming, Hornbill hopped closer and balanced precariously on a branch, still unused to his new tail.

"It's my tail!" he shrieked, pleading with the other monkeys to help. "The little white-nosed monkey tricked me and now he won't give me back my tail."

"But he won," one of the monkeys said.

"It's only right he keeps the tail as a prize," added another, which made the hornbill shriek again.

Hornbill's appeals to the monkeys were ignored, and they soon bounced away and out of his reach.

"But it's mine!" grunted Hornbill, his voice becoming hoarser. "Mine," he squawked, as his call became croakier.

The white-crested hornbill has been calling like this since that time when the drill monkeys were wise and the forest grew freely. He is still unable to accept that he was fooled, and still follows the monkeys, asking them to return his tail.

But he can never quite catch up with them.

Why the Bush Pig Digs Roots from the Ground

Tom Moorhouse

Bush Pig is the biggest grump in the Korup. We've all seen him snuffling around, with his scowly, jowly face, and his trotters and snout forever coated in dust. We've watched him digging and scraping and tusking and rootling and pootling and making big ruts in the ground. And when the rains come, he squelches and belches and snuffles and gruffles and bellows and wallows, and turns up clump after clump of claggy mud. And that's all he ever does.

But have you ever wondered what he's searching for, down there in the dirt? Well, it wouldn't be a good idea to ask him. Because if you do, he raises his head, fixes you with a piggy glare and grunts, "Mind your own business. Why are you disturbing me? Eh? Leave me be! Hah! Snufflegrunt!"

Then he turns his bristly back, shoves his snout to the dirt, and goes on his way.

But behind every grump lies a misfortune. (And before you judge anyone, you should remember that.) Some misfortunes are small and light, and a breeze can blow them from your shoulder. But others are large and heavy, and you carry them like a blanket on the hottest day. They fill your thoughts with their itchy heat and never leave you. It was a misfortune like this that once found Bush Pig.

Long ago, you see, back when all the animals were different, he had another name. In those days he was called Red River Hog, and he trotted through the bush with bright eyes, tidy bristles, his tusks polished and ears perked. And if you spoke to him, he inclined his head and answered politely, as was proper for the head of a fine and wealthy hoggish family. And while he had a bit of a temper (because no-one is perfect, not even you), if another animal needed money or a helping trotter, then all they had to do was ask. Red River Hog would always lend to a friend in need, and in all the eyes of Korup he was seen as the finest of beasts.

In all the eyes, that is, except the small, black unblinking eyes that belonged to Pa Tortoise. These eyes glinted each time Red River Hog trit-trotted past his house.

"That porker has plenty," said Pa Tortoise to his wife.

"Yes, he's a priceless pig," agreed Ma Tortoise.

"And it pains me to see him weighed down by wealth," said Pa Tortoise with a sly look. "I want to lighten his load."

Ma Tortoise frowned at her husband. "You leave that pig alone," she said. "Whatever you're scheming, it's sure to end badly."

"Humph, if you say so," said Pa Tortoise and left the house. But after two steps he muttered, "I'll have that hog's hoard." And after two more he said, "I'll swindle the swine!" He danced on the spot. "I'll pillage the pig!" he shouted. "The tortoise will be top!"

And Pa Tortoise rushed off to the clearing where he knew he would find Red River Hog. (It wouldn't look like rushing to you, but by the time he arrived in the clearing he was out of breath, and needed a snooze in the shade to recover.) And so, when some time later Red River Hog entered the clearing, he found Pa Tortoise gazing at a battered-looking patch of plants.

"Hello and good day to you, Uncle," called Red River Hog, trotting up to his friend.

Pa Tortoise blinked and turned from the plants. "Oh, it's you, Red River Hog," he said. "What a surprise to see you."

And Pa Tortoise looked as surprised as any tortoise could look who had been waiting in a clearing for three hours. Then he sighed, and turned away. "But I can't say that it's a good day. No, indeed I can't."

(And here I should tell you that although Pa Tortoise was staring at the plants, and pulling some of the glummest faces you've ever seen, out of the very most cornery corner of his eye he was watching Red River Hog as carefully as anyone has ever watched a pig. And that, as you know, is very carefully indeed.)

"Come on, Pa Tortoise, you can't be serious!" cried Red River Hog, with a concerned look around his tusks. "Snuffle. Grunt. The sun is shining, the shade is cool, and everything is good in Korup."

Pa Tortoise moaned. If you've ever heard anyone who ate too many kola nuts in one go, you will know the sort of moan he gave.

"Oh, if only that were true. But look, look at these plants."

Red River Hog looked. The plants were poorly. They were flat, as though someone had just finished trampling all over them. But of course nobody would do that, especially not Pa Tortoise who liked to eat there.

"These are my only food," groaned Pa Tortoise. "Oh, my poor Ma Tortoise will have nothing to eat!" He stifled a sob. "We've been so hungry! See how my flesh has wrinkled and my back has gone hard?" And Pa Tortoise raised a leg to show Red River Hog his wrinkly skin and shell. "And see how thin and beaky my lips have become?" As he raised his head, his beady eyes fixed on Red River Hog's face. "Don't you remember how I used to be, with my skin so plump and tight that it squeaked?"

Red River Hog didn't think he had ever heard Pa Tortoise squeak, but the tortoise was definitely very hard and wrinkly. So, being a kind pig, he said, "Snuffle. Of course I remember! It's terrible to see you like this. Snort. Why, you're wasting away! Snufflegrunt."

"I am," agreed Pa Tortoise. "But I could stand the aching in my belly, if it weren't for the thought of my poor, starving Ma Tortoise."

"Of course, of course," Red River Hog murmured, now feeling even more sorry for his friend.

"If only I could buy some seeds to plant," said Pa Tortoise. "And perhaps some mushrooms for my wife. And maybe a little fruit for myself. Oh, if I just had enough money to do that, then I'm sure my worries would be gone." He breathed his biggest and best sigh yet. "There would be no need for me to stand here, quietly starving to death."

And what could anyone do when faced with such a tale? Red River Hog dashed home and grabbed as many bags of his money as he could carry on his tusks. Then he galloped back to the clearing where Pa Tortoise was still staring at the plants. (They were now even flatter, as if somebody had been stamping on them a bit more.)

"Take these, take these. Snuffle," cried Red River Hog, dropping the bags in front of Pa Tortoise. "Grunt. No, don't refuse, my dear proud Tortoise. Just return the money when you can. Snort. It's enough to know that Ma Tortoise will have mushrooms for dinner. And don't thank me, I beg you. Snufflegrunt!"

Pa Tortoise took the money and promised to return it the moment that his seeds had grown. And Red River Hog went off home, saying things like, "It's just as well I was there to help."

Now, everyone knows (and you know it, don't you?) that lending money is like spilling water from your hands. Trickle it onto the right soil and fruit and grain will grow, enough to fill everyone's belly. But in other places the earth is deep and thirsty and guzzles water by the cup, the jug, the bucket. Only the bitter weeds of regret and anger will ever grow in such earth, and there they grow strong. Their shoots spring out, grab your feet, twist up your legs and bind you to misery. And, as all the animals knew (except poor Red River Hog), the thirstiest, weediest, most miserable ground in all Korup belonged to Pa Tortoise.

So it was, days later, that Red River Hog found himself gazing at his small amount of remaining money. *My wealth has gone to a good cause*, he thought (without snuffling or grunting, because these are thoughts and thoughts don't snuffle), *but I can't help wishing that I hadn't given so much of it away. I must have given Pa Tortoise ten times what he needs for seeds and now there isn't much left for me.*

Being a practical pig, and swallowing his pride, Red River Hog went to Pa Tortoise's house and asked – and he was so sorry for asking, snuffle, but he found himself, well, grunt, a bit short of cash – if Pa Tortoise would be able to give back some of the borrowed money?

"Of course, as soon as I can," replied Pa Tortoise. "I just can't today because my mushrooms are drooping and I'm worried about them."

And who could argue with that? But when Red River Hog came the next day, he found that the money couldn't be returned because, as Pa Tortoise said, "My wife sneezed three times at breakfast and everyone knows that's bad luck. I wouldn't be your friend if I gave you ill-omened money."

Which was fair enough. And the next day, unfortunately, Pa Tortoise's shell had become too tight, and he needed to see the doctor to have it loosened. And the next day the sun was too shiny, and then the moon too white and the sky too blue. And as the days became weeks and the weeks months, the trees were always too leafy, or the dust too dusty or the air too airy for Pa Tortoise to return the money.

Meanwhile, Red River Hog became a sorry-looking animal. He grew hungry and thin. He moped around with hair unbrushed and tusks unpolished, and his ribs sticking out against his coat. And as he passed though the bush, some animals turned aside, sniggering – for there are always those who will mock others' misfortune. (Wiser animals, though, kept quiet, and were glad that they had not been so badly treated. And this too is something to learn.) And slowly the thought formed in his mind that maybe, just maybe, people were laughing at him. And maybe – yes, perhaps this really was the reason – it was because the tortoise was making him look like an idiot.

Now, do you remember how I said that regret and anger sprout from thirsty ground and tie you to misery? Good, because that is what happened to Red River Hog. The shoots grabbed him, twisted all up his body, wormed in through his ears and entered his heart. And there they tightened and clenched. And now he seethed by day and snarled by night. He went to bed fuming and dreamed of jumping up and down on tortoises. He woke every morning raging, and stamped about with brows lowered, nostrils flaring and teeth grinding. He bore it as long as he could, until one morning he leapt from his bed with a snarling snort. He bawled a belligerent bellow. He hollered a horrible howl. Then he dashed from his door and pounded down the path to the Tortoises' house.

Some distance away, Pa Tortoise was standing in his own front garden thinking about how nice it was to have lots of money, when the forest fell strangely silent. A hush rolled across Korup, as if all of the animals had suddenly decided to keep very, very quiet. A bird shot up from a distant tree. Then another, and another. Then a whole flock leapt from the branches, flapping for their lives. And at the edge of hearing, Pa Tortoise heard a low rumble, followed by a crashing, then

a smashing, a thrashing and a mashing. And then, in a whirl of twigs, leaves and branches, the angriest hog Korup had ever seen hurtled from the bush. He skidded to a stop in Pa Tortoise's garden, and his trotters tore great gouges from the ground.

"WHERE'S THAT SNARFLESNARL TORTOISE?" he roared. (For Pa Tortoise was no longer in the garden. Moving faster than a tortoise ever did before, or has since, he was now cowering in the kitchen.) Red River Hog's eyes were red and clouds of steam rose from his flanks. It was not a sight to fill a tortoise with the expectation of a long and happy life.

"Tortoise, bring me my money or I'll rip you from your shell!" yelled Red River Hog.

"The pig's possessed!" hissed Pa Tortoise to his wife. "The boar's gone bananas, the hog's lost his head!" His face was filled with terror. "He'll trample me with trotters. He'll tear me with tusks!" He started to wail. "Oh what am I to do?"

Ma Tortoise looked up from the chilli peppers she was grinding for dinner. "Don't worry, he won't gore you." Her black eyes twinkled with mirth. "Just do exactly as I say. Now quickly, pull in your head and legs."

Quick as a fairly fast flash, Pa Tortoise yanked his head and legs down deep into his shell. And now he looked like a big, brown-green rock.

"Right," said Ma Tortoise, whispering down the hole where her husband's head had been, "let me do the talking and no matter what happens, don't come out until I call your name." Then she flipped Pa Tortoise onto his back and began to rock him across the peppers, using him like a grindstone.

An immense battering rang through the house. The front door splintered to pieces, and Red River Hog leapt through the shattered frame. He flung himself, snorting, into the room.

"The door's open, come in," said Ma Tortoise, not looking up from grinding her peppers (using Pa Tortoise).

Red River Hog was in no mood to be polite. He kicked the wall and stomped on the floor and charged around in a tantrum. "I snortgruffle have snortsnort come for my hargsnortle money," he yelled. "Where is that gruntleharg tortoise? Where is my snufflegrunt money? Hah?"

"Well, I'm not exactly sure," said Ma Tortoise, still grinding. "My husband takes care of business, and he's not home."

"Not GRUNTLESNORT home?" thundered Red River Hog. "Not SNORTLE here? I saw him come in! I'll give you not SNUFFLEGRUNT home!"

Red River Hog lost his temper once and for all. He lashed out with his trotters and kicked the grindstone from Mrs Tortoise's grip. It flew straight out of a window and landed with a crack in the yard. (It also said "Ouch," but luckily for Pa Tortoise, Red River Hog was too angry to hear it.)

Ma Tortoise gave Red River Hog a stern and disapproving look. (It was the type of look that only Ma Tortoise can give, and you really wouldn't want to see it.)

"Now you listen to me," she said. "I don't know what business you have with Pa Tortoise," and on these last two words she raised her voice, so that Pa Tortoise – who was still spinning to a stop outside – would hear her calling his name, "but no nice gentleman would charge around the way you do. Honestly, what a way to behave!"

Under Ma Tortoise's stare, Red River Hog began to look a bit bashful.

"It's a disgrace!" said Ma Tortoise, and Red River Hog looked embarrassed. "He bursts into my house and kicks the grindstone from my very grasp. What's the world coming to?"

And she tutted in a way that made Red River Hog swallow and mumble something like, "I'm so very snufflegruntsnort sorry."

"That's very well for you to say," said Ma Tortoise, "but you have just kicked my most precious grindstone into the yard. My poor departed mother left me that stone."

Red River Hog hung his head.

"Now," commanded Ma Tortoise (and if Red River Hog had been in any condition to notice, he would have seen triumph in her eye), "get out there and fetch my grindstone. And don't think that you're getting a penny of your money until it's returned. Understand?"

Red River Hog said sorry, and of course that was fair, and that he would, with a great snuffle and perhaps a grunt or two, head out immediately and bring back the grindstone. And he slunk from the house to retrieve it.

But when Red River Hog arrived at the place where the grindstone had landed, it was nowhere to be seen. It had vanished. (Because Pa Tortoise, hearing his name called, had run to the back door before Red River Hog could find him.)

And although Red River Hog snuffled here and gruntled there and rootled and pootled as only he could, he found no trace of the missing stone. In the end, he gave up and went back to the Tortoises' house. He said to Ma Tortoise in a small voice, "I'm terribly sorry. Snuffle. But I can't find your grindstone. Grunt."

At that moment, Pa Tortoise wandered into the room. He grinned at Red River Hog, gave his wife a sly wink and said, "Well, here's a nice surprise!" (And he looked as surprised as any tortoise can look when he's just been kicked out of a window by a pig.) "It's good luck that you dropped in because I have all of your money here and I'm ready to give it back."

"But he won't see a coin of it," Ma Tortoise snapped. "Not until he returns my grindstone. That's what he said."

"But it wasn't there," said Red River Hog, giving her a pleading look. "I couldn't find it."

"Not a penny, then," said Ma Tortoise.

And what could Red River Hog do? He had definitely kicked the grindstone. And it was definitely gone. And all his bags of wealth definitely depended on him finding it. He gazed in desperation from tortoise to pitiless tortoise, but saw no hope for his money. And so he fled from their house and disappeared into the bush, all of a sob and a snuffle, with his eyes locked on the ground as he hunted for the grindstone.

So now you know why Red River Hog goes around with his snout in the dirt: he's looking for a grindstone that he will never find. He doesn't know, poor beast, that his money's as good as gone. The other animals tried to tell him so, but he always replied, "Hah! Mind your own business. Snufflegrunt!"

So after a while they gave up and forgot his name. To them he became merely a pig in the bush, and they called him "Bush Pig".

Ah, poor unlucky Bush Pig. But you know that anything that happens to one can always happen to others. So if you're not careful, you too could find yourself snuffling around with lost wealth and a different name. And if you learn anything from this story, maybe it should be to think twice before judging even the grouchiest of grumps – and at least thrice before lending a single coin to a terrible trickster tortoise.

How the Fly Defeats the Elephant

Geraldine McCaughrean

"Blaah! Blaah! Elefunk goes trunkety trunk!"

The whole forest shook when Pa Elephant arrived. It shook because he trumpeted so loudly. It shook because he was so huge, and his feet thump-thump-thumped. But most of all, the forest shook from fear, because Pa Elephant was such a bully.

He pushed over the giraffes. He stomped on the ant nests. He slapped the bongo on her striped bottom with his trunk. He picked up the long-tailed pangolin by his long tail and whirled him round in the air. He squirted dirty water over the lovely plumes of the sunbird.

Behind his back, the animals all said:

"I don't like that Elephant."

"He's a bad sort."

"I wish he would fall in a very deep hole and never get out."

But when he was standing there, lower lip pushed out, tusks shining, and his big ears spread like the sails of a ship, they bowed and smiled and said:

"Yes, Uncle."

"No, Uncle."

"Certainly, Uncle."

"How are you today, Uncle?"

One part of Elephant was even bigger than his ears, and that was his pride. He thought he was better and braver and fiercer than anyone else in the forest. Now and then, he challenged someone to fight him – the colobus monkey or the bush pig or the bushbuck. When this happened, the colobus suddenly found something important to do up a tree. The bush pig dug a hole and put his head down it. The bushbuck pretended to practice his jumping, jumped over a bush and did not come out again.

Everyone knew that Elephant was too big to beat. But then, when no one would fight him, he called them cowards and weaklings and blew in their faces: "Blaaaaaaah!"

Elephant liked to make everyone feel small.

He could not make Ma Fly feel small. Fly was small already, and she knew it.

"What a pointless creature you are," said Elephant. "You look like a full stop. You look like an apple pip. You look like a speck of mud that flies up when I splash through a puddle."

"Thank you, Uncle," said Fly politely. "How kind of you. It is just as well I look so foolish. If everyone knew how *strong* I am, they might be afraid…and I do not want to frighten anyone."

"*STRONG?!*" blared Elephant. "I could stamp on you and no one would ever find the bits! Now buzz off!" And he laughed so loud that kola nuts fell out of the trees.

"If you don't believe me, let's fight," said Fly softly. "A friendly fight."

Elephant looked around him. All the other animals were staring and whispering.

"Ridiculous blip," he said. "I will swat you all the way from today into the middle of next week. We fight this evening!"

Now the forest shook with excitement. Birds were swooping this way and that, spreading the news. Chimpanzees were whooping through the treetops – *Come look! Come see! Fly and Elephant are going to fight!*

Of course, everyone wanted Ma Fly to win. But they dared not say so. Anyway, how was that possible, Fly being so tiny? So when Elephant arrived for the contest, scared little voices greeted him:

"Big is best!"
"Pa Elephant rules!"
"Go, Uncle!"

When Fly flew in, they fell silent.

In a clean clearing, on a brown round of ground, Elephant and Fly began to fight. That is to say, Elephant kicked and stomped. He twirled his trunk. He thrust out his tusks. Fly dodged about.

Elephant jumped with all four feet on the spot where Fly was standing. But Fly simply took off.

Elephant flapped and clapped his ears together, fit to

flatten Fly. But Fly only flew into Elephant's little ear hole...and *buzzzzzzed.* She tickled, she squiggled, and she *buzzzzzed.*

Elephant shook his head till he was dizzy. *Buzz buzz buzzz.* Elephant rubbed his head along the ground, but still: *buzz buzz buzzz.*

Elephant scratched his ear against a tree until the tree fell over. But still: *buzz buzz buzzz.*

The other animals watched open-mouthed as Elephant rolled and bellowed and danced about and the (quite invisible) Fly tickled and squiggled and *buzzed.*

Elephant put the tip of his trunk in his ear and squirted, but still: *buzz buzz buzzz.*

Elephant stood on his head, hoping Fly would drop out, but still: *buzz buzz buzzz.*

Soon, the other animals began to cheer and laugh. They sent their wives home to fetch the children to come and see Pa Elephant fighting Ma Fly. All afternoon, Elephant tried to be rid of the *buzz buzz buzzing* in his ear. Weary and wearier, grubby and grubbier he grew, until he was completely worn out. He lay splayed out on the brown ground, a dusty, dirty heap of sorrow.

"Oh come out, do! Do come out, you!" begged Elephant.

"You who?"

"You, Aunty," said Elephant. "Pleeeease."

"I will come out on one condition: if you promise never to bully anyone ever again."

"Me? A bully? I never…"

Buzzz. Buzzzz.

"I promise! I promise!"

So Ma Fly crawled out of Elephant's ear and stood on his forehead, while the animals clapped and cheered and sang:

"Hoorah for flies, and we'll tell you why.
They're clever and wise, no matter their size.
Flies will surprise you; believe your eyes, you.
Fly won the prize, so hoorah for flies!"

Pa Elephant was true to his word. If sometimes he forgets and starts to stomp and trumpet and pick on some animal smaller than he, up pops Fly and circles his head humming: *Buzzz. Buzzz.*

Then Elephant suddenly remembers his manners.

Now the animals in the forest are far happier than before. Even Elephant.

Since he started being kinder to his neighbours, he has found they like him better. They tell him their news. They tell him jokes and stories. They ask his advice and invite him home to tea (though he doesn't often fit). The bongo even wanted to name her child after him – 'Pa Elephant' – but everyone said that would be too confusing.

Why the Drill Monkey has a Blue Bottom

Beverley Naidoo

In the middle of the forest was a village where all the animals shared everything. When there was a feast, everyone was invited. When there was a wedding, everyone came to dance. When a baby was born, everyone brought presents. O-oo, everyone said that it was a good village.

Did I say *everyone*?

I mean everyone from that village and the forest around it. You see, when there was a feast or a wedding or a new baby, the invitation passed quickly from one villager to another. Then the birds carried the invitation to other animals in the forest nearby.

But there was one place where the birds did not fly. This was the place where Pa Tortoise lived. They said that Tortoise had fast hands that made things disappear. They said that he was too good at tricks. Every bird in the forest had a story about Tortoise and you know how birds like to chatter.

Chit-chat-chit-chat! Chit-chat-chit-chat!

Now, Tortoise knew that the animals and birds didn't want to invite him to their village.

"They envy me," he said to himself. "They know I have a good skull! Is it my fault if others are not as clever as I am?"

Tortoise also remembered the time when he had been made to jump from high in the sky! O-oo, he still had the dents on his back. If you want to know the truth, Tortoise was very upset that he was not welcome in the village.

Well, my story begins on a day when there was no feast and there was no wedding. But on this day, Ma Hen had been sitting for a long time on six beautiful brown eggs. She had made her roost inside the hollow of a huge old rotten Zebrawood tree, right in the middle of the village. Everyone who passed by stopped to ask how she was.

"Good day!" everyone said to Ma Hen.

"O-oo! Yes, it's a good day!" said Ma Hen. "Soon you will see my six beautiful chicks."

Ma Hen said this over and over again. Everyone waited... and waited. But still no chicks appeared. Poor Ma Hen. None of her eggs would hatch.

Now, everyone liked Ma Hen and they felt very sorry for her.

"We must have a meeting. We must find a way to help Ma Hen," said Ma Hornbill. "We don't like to see our friend so sad."

So the villagers called a meeting in the market-place. There was a lot of talk among all the animals, and the birds made a lot of chatter.

Chit-chat-chit-chat! Chit-chat-chit-chat!

Even Pa Elephant came to have his say. He said he wished he could help, but if he tried to hatch the eggs, he might crush them. Everyone agreed that it was not a good idea for such a big animal to sit on them.

"I wish that I could help," said Ma Drill, "but the eggs are small and I am also too big. We need someone who is the right size."

"Well, how about you, Ma Hornbill?" asked Pa Drill, who sat next to his wife on a large stone. "You are the right size. Maybe you could hatch them?"

"I would like to help," said Ma Hornbill, "but my own chicks need me. My husband is looking after them for me and I can't leave them for too long." She shook her long yellow beak. "Sorry, sorry!" said Ma Hornbill as she stretched her wings and flew away.

Well, one by one, every bird and animal said why they couldn't help Ma Hen.

"This is very sad," said Ma Drill. "One of us will have to go and tell our poor friend."

Now, at that very moment, a new voice spoke. It came from behind the red trunk of an iroko tree.

"Can I help?" said the voice.

Everyone turned to see who it was. O-oo, it was Tortoise.

"I have listened to you all," said Tortoise. "I can help Ma Hen. I am just the right size. We tortoises know all about eggs and how to hatch them."

The animals and the birds looked at each other. What should they do? None of them could help Ma Hen and here was Pa Tortoise saying that he could do the job. Pa Elephant was the first to speak.

"How can we be sure that you know what you are doing?" Pa Elephant swung his trunk, waiting for a reply.

Tortoise felt cross at how Pa Elephant spoke to him. But he was too clever to show his feelings.

"I need to go home to bring something that will help," said Tortoise. "I shall come back tomorrow morning. But you must have ready for me a very hot flat stone, some oil, salt and a lot of spices."

Well, some of the animals and birds were surprised. Why did Tortoise need these things? But Tortoise looked so cool and sure of himself that even Pa Elephant didn't ask him to explain. He didn't want to look foolish and nor did anyone else. So they agreed to have the very hot stone, oil, salt and spices ready for the next day.

"I shall see you tomorrow," said Tortoise, and he walked away into the forest, slowly and surely.

The next morning, as the birds began to sing their morning songs, Tortoise returned to the village and made his way to Ma Hen's roost. All the animals and birds were waiting there. Ma Hen came to the entrance of the hollow. In front of the old Zebrawood tree were the flat stone, the oil, salt and spices. They had even made a small fire to keep the stone piping hot.

"Very good," said Tortoise. "As you can see, I have also

brought something special to help me." He lifted up a large bag woven with leaves.

Now, no one could tell what was inside the bag and no one dared to ask. Perhaps it was something magic and Tortoise would be angry. Everyone waited quietly. Only Ma Hen clucked softly. At last she would see her six chicks!

"Very good," Tortoise said again. I shall now go into the roost and hang up my bag over the entrance. Everyone else must stay outside here."

"Can I not stay inside with you?" begged Ma Hen.

"No," said Tortoise. "If you want me to hatch your eggs, everyone must stay outside, even you." Then he pointed to a small hole near the top of his bag.

"Every time that I hatch an egg," said Tortoise, "I shall bring the chick to this hole and show it to you. You can count the chicks until there are six. But if anyone moves the bag to come inside, the eggs will not hatch. Is that clear?"

One by one, everyone nodded. The last one to nod was Ma Hen. After that, Tortoise picked up the oil, salt and spices and placed them inside the roost. Then, careful not to burn himself, he swiftly moved the hot stone into the roost and hung the bag woven with leaves across the entrance.

Now, what was inside Tortoise's bag? If the animals and birds had looked very carefully, they might have seen it move a little.

Tortoise quickly got to work. First, he poured a little oil onto the hot stone. Then he opened his bag and took out a little day-old chick that he had carried all the way from his home. He lifted the chick to the peep-hole and called through the door.

"My friends! See, here is the first chick!"

Ma Hen clucked loudly and everyone clapped and cheered. The animals and birds began singing and dancing and, at the same time, Tortoise cracked open the first egg. Of course you know what he did next. He cooked it with salt and spices in the oil. Everyone made so much noise outside that no one heard any crackling or sizzling.

Once again, Tortoise took his day-old chick to the peep-hole and there was new clapping, cheering, singing and dancing around happy Ma Hen. So Tortoise cracked open the next egg... then the next and the next until he had shown his day-old chick six times. It wasn't very long before he had cooked and eaten all six of Ma Hen's eggs. Then he put his chick back in his bag and got ready to leave. O-oo, he was so fat and full!

As soon as Tortoise appeared at the entrance, everyone cheered and clapped again. They pointed to a pile of bush mangoes, bananas, pawpaws and yams.

"Thank you, thank you! These are presents for you to take home!"

Tortoise's eyes lit up as he pulled his bag behind him across the entrance. He smiled as Ma Hen hurried forward.

"I have been happy to help but there is one more thing you need to do," said Tortoise. "Your chicks are fine, Ma Hen. But you must leave them alone until the sun is right above you. It won't be long but if you go in now, I am afraid that your chicks will die."

Poor Ma Hen! What should she do? She wanted to see her chicks right away but she was frightened by Tortoise's warning. Indeed, all the animals were frightened by the warning and became quiet.

"Thank you for my presents," said Tortoise. "But I need help to carry them home. As you know, I am slow and I am already late."

The animals did not want to seem ungrateful.

"I can help you," said Pa Drill. "You can climb on my back but, first, let us put the presents into your bag."

"Thank you," said Tortoise. "But can you give me another bag for them? I shall leave my own bag here for Ma Hen."

So Ma Drill found another bag, and Pa Elephant used his trunk to fill it up with the fruit and vegetables. No one thought it strange when Tortoise said he needed to check that he hadn't left anything behind and went back into the roost. After all, the special things he had brought with him had helped him hatch the chicks. (Of course, Tortoise wanted to take back the little chick that he had brought from home!) Nor did anyone think it strange when a few moments later he slipped something into the bag full of presents. Everyone gave one last cheer as Tortoise jumped onto Pa Drill's back.

"Let's go!" he called out. Then he pointed through the treetops to the sky. "See, the sun will soon be above your village!"

Ma Hen and all the other animals looked up as Pa Drill disappeared into the forest with Tortoise and his presents.

As soon as the sun was directly above the village, Ma Hen entered her roost. Her friends waited outside so they could hear her happy clucking. Instead, they heard the most terrible squawking and screeching. Pushing aside Tortoise's bag, they rushed inside. There were no little yellow chicks. There was only Ma Hen running round and round, pecking at a pile of broken egg shells. Tortoise had cheated them! What fools he had made of them all!

Well, the animals were so angry that they began to chase after Pa Drill and Tortoise. Pa Elephant led the way, crashing between the trees of the forest. As soon as Tortoise heard the sound, he knew what it was and he started to sing a song about Pa Drill. He sang so loudly that Pa Drill couldn't hear the shouts for them to come back:

Pa Drill is the fastest!
Pa Drill is the best!
Don't be surprised
that Ma Drill is impressed!

Pa Drill laughed and the faster and louder that Tortoise sang, the faster he ran.

Now, Tortoise didn't want Pa Drill to see where he lived so when Tortoise could no longer hear any shouting, he stopped singing.

"This is where I store my food," he told Pa Drill. "Leave me here and I will sort my fine presents. You must want to get back to your village feast."

"I shall sing the song to my wife!" said Pa Drill. "I know that she will like it." With that, Pa Drill thanked Tortoise again, said goodbye, and set off home.

Can you imagine what happened next? Pa Drill thought that everyone would be enjoying a feast with more singing and dancing in the village. He wanted to sing Tortoise's song to everyone! But when he arrived, there was no singing and dancing. Instead, Pa Drill found a crowd of angry faces. Nearly everyone was waving a branch from a tree. Only Ma Drill didn't have a branch and she looked very worried.

"Why didn't you stop when we called you?" Pa Elephant raised his trunk and let out a great blast of air.

"But I didn't hear anyone calling," said Pa Drill. "Tortoise made up a song about me. He sang it very loudly as I carried him through the forest."

"Come and see what your Tortoise friend did!" boomed Pa Elephant. He flapped his huge ears and led Pa Drill to Ma Hen's roost. As soon as he saw Ma Hen crying and clucking over the broken egg shells, Pa Drill understood. Tortoise had cheated them and everyone blamed him for helping Tortoise to escape.

When he came out of Ma Hen's roost, Pa Drill saw the animals and birds all lined up, on each side, with their branches raised. He ran as fast as he could, and his stinging bottom made him run even faster. As he ran into the forest, Ma Drill joined him. Some of the animals kept on following. When they finally stopped, Ma and Pa Drill were alone. They knew that things would never be the same again in the village.

People say that was the day when Ma and Pa Drill's bottoms turned blue. They are still blue today.

So that is the end of my story. But I have a question. If the animals and birds of the village had shared their feasts and weddings with Tortoise, would he still have played this terrible trick? I hand this question over to you!

How the Monkey Defeats the Crocodile

Piers Torday

Another day dawned in Korup. Sunlight spread out across the endless, undulating canopy of the jungle, the thousand different greens and browns of the giant trees that sheltered the river Mana below, lianas looping down into the water as it sluggishly slid past. A warbler welcomed the new morning with his merry song. Brightly-coloured tree mice and frogs replied in chorus from the trunks beneath.

And, on the very bottom of the forest floor, Ma Pangolin dared poke her snout up above a pile of leaves, keeping a lookout for a very dear friend. She watched as, his little black face twitching under a pair of bushy eyebrows, a monkey picked his way down through the white flowers of a milkwood tree towards her.

Pa Colobus.

Now, this monkey was no ordinary monkey. He wasn't the leader of his troop. He wasn't that big or strong. He wasn't even very handsome. But there was not a smarter colobus to be found along the banks of the Mana.

At least, that was what Ma Pangolin always told him, because she liked to look out for her friends and encourage them. She just didn't always expect them to believe every word...

Now, what Pa Colobus wanted most at the start of another long, dry day was a deep, refreshing drink. He didn't even stop to greet Pangolin properly, but padded down past her towards the muddy shore of the river. Because he was a very clever monkey, he took care not to get too close in case there was anyone unfriendly waiting in the water.

Like a crocodile.

Exactly like the crocodile that rose out of the river just then, his jaws dripping with water. Colobus leapt into the air, grabbing at a branch – because, although he was clever, he was also easily scared. But the crocodile did not snap after the monkey. Instead he just shook his head, smiling.

"Good afternoon, Pa Colobus," said the crocodile.

"Good afternoon, Pa Crocodile," said the monkey, clinging to the branch. "You don't want to eat me, do you?"

"Now why would I want to do a thing like that?" said Crocodile, flashing his sharp teeth again.

"Because you're a crocodile?"

"That's a little unfair on crocodiles, don't you think?" said the crocodile. "I was only being friendly."

Colobus wrinkled his nose. In his experience, crocodiles were never that friendly. "Prove it," he said, still gripping the tree. "If you want to be my friend, prove it."

"I will," said Crocodile. "But first, tell me your favourite colour."

What's that got to do with anything? thought Colobus, but he told him anyway. "The silver of the moon."

"Wait right there," said Crocodile and, with a flick of his tail, he was gone. There were only a few bubbles on the surface to show he had ever been there.

Colobus waited for a moment until he was certain the crocodile had gone, and dropped down from the tree. His fur seemed to almost float behind him, and he landed as softly as a leaf upon the river bank. Ignoring Pangolin's muttered warnings, he approached the water again and began to drink.

He hadn't had much more than a mouthful when two slitted eyes reappeared right in front of him. They were so near, Colobus could see the veins in the eyeballs. He was so scared he didn't dare move a single hair of that beautiful fur.

"Hello," gulped the monkey, eyes wide with terror.

"I brought you a present," said Crocodile, still fixing the monkey with his strange grin.

"What kind of present?" said Colobus.

"A beautiful one!" The crocodile's great tail rose out of the water, dark and dripping. Colobus flinched, but then he saw what was clasped tightly in its curled tip.

A large silver fish, which flashed in the light.

Crocodile laid the gift at Colobus's feet. The monkey did not eat silver fish, but he thought it a beautiful present and was pleased, pretending not to notice the pangolin who was in a sulk at being ignored and digging an ostentatiously large hole in the sand.

"Now it's my turn," he said, because he was a polite and well brought up monkey – as well as a clever one.

Pa Colobus scrambled back up into the trees. He climbed higher and higher, leaping from branch to branch. Finally, he got to the top of the tallest iroko tree in the jungle – nearly as tall as Mount Yuhan itself. Poking his head out above the canopy, he saw the many treetops of the jungle stretching out before him underneath a baking blue crescent of sky. This dry season had gone on forever. He wondered if it was ever going to rain again. He took a deep breath and then dived back down.

It did not take him long to find what he was looking for.

Just a few jumps and swings later, he was back on the riverbank. At first, it looked deserted, and he thought Crocodile had disappeared. But the funny thing was, as soon as his paws touched the ground, the reptile rose up from the slow brown water where he had been waiting.

"Oh, there you are!" said Colobus. "I brought you a present."

And he pulled out from the folds of his fur a bunch of yellow-green fruit, almost the same colour as the crocodile's pale belly. There was plenty of this fruit sticking out from umbrella trees high up in the jungle, but the crocodile had never seen any before and his eyes widened.

"Thank you very much," he said – and ate the fruit. (Because that was what crocodiles mainly liked to do. Eat things.)

"My turn again," he said, and dived below the surface once more. This time, the monkey did not have to wait long. In a few minutes, the crocodile reappeared with a long bit of wood between his teeth. It had an oval leaf-shaped bit at the end, and looked old and rotten. Colobus half-recognised the piece of wood. Where had he seen one of those before?

"What's that?" he asked, jabbing at it with his finger.

Crocodile gave a crocodile shrug. "I don't know," he said, "but I thought you might have more use for it than I."

"Hmm," said the monkey, rubbing his whiskery chin. "Where did you get it?"

"I found it," said Pa Crocodile, with a big dripping smile.

Then the monkey realised, clapping his palm to his head with excitement. "I know what it is! It's one of those things Man uses when he floats down the river in those hollowed-out logs. He doesn't have flippers or tails so he makes these instead."

"Maybe," said the crocodile, with a chuckle. Watching from behind a mango bush, Ma Pangolin sighed. This was not going to end well.

Still, Pa Colobus chuckled too. Somehow, when a crocodile chuckled, it was hard not to chuckle along. Then they chuckled some more. Then some more, till they both nearly split their sides.

And the monkey took the paddle (for that was what it was) and tapped the crocodile on the nose.

Crocodile stopped laughing.

Colobus froze.

After a few tense moments, the crocodile tapped the monkey back with his tail. "There!" he said, and they began laughing all over again.

"Well," said the monkey, wiping his brow. "This has been a most unexpected morning. It was good to meet you, Pa Crocodile."

"And you, Pa Colobus. Same time, same place, tomorrow?"

This is exactly what they agreed. The following morning, Colobus came down with a large bunch of iroko leaves for his friend. Crocodile explained that he didn't eat leaves, and then they were so busy laughing again, the monkey clean forgot to ask what he *did* eat. Then the day after that, Crocodile gave Colobus a present of a wash, by thrashing his tail in the water and soaking the monkey from top to bottom. They laughed, played, splashed and became the firmest of friends – as well as spotlessly clean.

From then on, they met every morning, just by the same spot beneath the milkwood tree, on the shore of the old deep river that had been sliding past that tree for hundreds of years.

But then, one day, Colobus came flying down through the trees to their usual meeting spot, and there was no sign of the crocodile.

"Hello!" he called out across the water, cupping his hands over his mouth. "Pa Crocodile! It's me, your friend, Pa Colobus. I have brought you the most delicious pineapple you have ever laid your eyes on." And he had. Clasped firmly against his chest was the most golden, spiky pineapple you have ever seen. It looked like an incredible giant jewel. The monkey sat with his jewel by the bank and waited for his friend to arrive.

But no Crocodile came. Only the pangolin, watching over her friend through some long grasses.

Night did arrive, however, followed not long after by the next day.

Pa Colobus woke with a start, finding himself still sitting on the bank of the river. He sprang into the air, clutching his precious pineapple. "Who goes there?" he demanded. But it was only the sun. Then the next day passed, and the one after that, and then, before he knew it, a whole week had gone by without any sign of the crocodile. And the monkey got so hungry, he actually ate his friend's present. (With a bit of help from Pangolin, naturally.)

Finally, Colobus gave up. He was beginning to worry that if he stayed there any longer, he might become a tempting snack for a passing chimp. His head low, he began to make his way back through the trees, when there was a little splash behind him.

He turned around and was overjoyed to see Crocodile. Immediately, he knew something was wrong. The crocodile's eyes were soft and sad, and he was not even smiling. Crocodiles were always smiling. He knew this had to be bad.

"Pa Crocodile!" he exclaimed. "Wherever have you been? What can be the matter? I thought you had gone away. Maybe I did something, maybe I said something? Did you not like the last present I gave you –"

His friend shook his long dark snout in the water and lowered his eyes.

"No, Pa Colobus, it is nothing you have done."

"Then what!"

Crocodile looked up and a single fat tear rolled down his cheeks into the river. Colobus gasped. He had never seen a crocodile cry about anything before. (Monkeys cried all the time. Especially if someone stole their banana.)

The crocodile continued. "My father is gravely ill. I have been away looking after him."

Now Colobus was not confused, but sad for the crocodile. "I am so sorry to hear this. What is the problem? Have you seen a doctor?"

"Yes, I have. One of the finest crocodile consultants there is. He has his own private cave and everything. Super expensive, but it can't be helped. This is my father we're talking about after all!"

Colobus nodded sympathetically, but Pangolin rubbed her snout with suspicion.

"He has recommended a course of herbs for him to go on," continued Crocodile. "Hopefully my insurance will cover it."

"If there is anything I can do... Would you like me to maybe go into the jungle and find some herbs for you?"

His friend shook his large crocodile head. "You are most kind, Pa Colobus. Thank you, but there is no need. You are such a good friend. It means so much at this difficult time." Crocodile smiled. "Who would have thought it – a monkey and a crocodile being such good friends?"

"I know," said the monkey. "But we are, aren't we? We get along so well."

"We do," agreed the crocodile.

Colobus nodded with satisfaction and they sat there for a moment, watching a dragonfly dart about in the shallows.

"And on that point," coughed Crocodile, "I was actually wondering if there was something you could do for me to help my poor father."

"Anything, dear friend," said Colobus. "Anything at all! You only have to ask."

"Well," said the crocodile, and imperceptibly – the dark bulk of his body concealed by the water – he slid closer to where the monkey was sitting on the shore. "I was wondering, would you be able to pay me a visit at my home?"

Here Colobus had to pause for a moment. He studied his reflection in the brown water. He looked at his eyes, his nose, his lips and his thumb-free hands. There was no two ways about it – he was definitely a monkey. Casting his eyes across, he could see that – beyond all possible doubt – his great friend was definitely a crocodile.

The sad truth was that crocodiles didn't have many friends in the jungle. Certainly not ones they invited back to their home. Because – that just wouldn't be sensible, would it? Not when their homes were often deep under water, and often full of, well...their food.

"So?" said Crocodile in his smooth, deep voice, which was as mellow as the velvety darkness of midnight. "What do you think?"

"Ah, well, you see," stammered Colobus, looking around desperately for an excuse. "It's sweet of you to ask, and I would love to come, but..."

"But what?"

The monkey's eyes scanned the riverbank frantically, dreaming up polite ways to refuse an invitation from a crocodile. He saw Pangolin, who jabbed at the thing she was standing next to.

"Because...I'm turning into a tree!"

"A tree. You're turning into a tree."

"Yes...so I couldn't possibly, you see...I would be too...you know, wooden. Branches would get in the way. So sorry."

"And when exactly are you...turning into a tree?"

"Now...I mean, tomorrow! On Thursday. Next week." The monkey realised he hadn't actually asked the crocodile when he should visit his home.

"That's fine then," said Crocodile, "because my invitation is for Wednesday, today, this week. So why don't you jump on my back now, and I'll take you there directly."

His friend gulped, and began to sweat even more than normal. He looked wildly around him and spotted Pangolin, who was doing her best to keep out of the way, snuffling along in her armoured scales beneath a line of ferns. Colobus lunged out and grabbed the poor creature, pressing her to his breast.

"I can't do that," he declared. "Ma Pangolin and I...well, I wanted you to be the first to know...we're getting married."

Pangolin looked as surprised as a pangolin can look (which isn't very), while the crocodile's eyes narrowed to a scary slit. "You're getting married to a pangolin?" he hissed.

"Yes," squeaked Colobus. "Now. Right this second. I wanted you to be the first to know. But we need to go now...choose a dress, all that kind of thing, when will it ever end..." He began to edge back up the shore, holding the pangolin tight and kissing her head all the while – much to Pangolin's disgust.

Crocodile thrashed his tail in the water, soaking them all. Pangolin seized the moment to spring free from the monkey's arms and into a bush, where she lay, quivering.

"I thought you were my friend," said the crocodile, his lower lip trembling. "My father is dying!"

A large salty tear rolled down his wrinkled face.

Colobus felt ashamed. "In that case, I accept your kind invitation."

And he jumped onto the crocodile's back.

As they glided down the river – or at least, the crocodile glided, while the monkey tried to keep his balance and the pangolin skidded after them – the green walls of jungle slowly gave way to more open river bank, mud caked rocks and a sandy shoreline.

Just ahead of them, draped over those rocks – like he had been put out to dry – was a much bigger crocodile than his friend. A much older one too – his features were harder, his belly grey and shrunken.

Pangolin crept out from under a large leaf and watched anxiously, her paws half over her eyes because, if she knew anything, she knew that monkeys and crocodiles were not destined to be friends.

"Is that your father?" whispered Colobus, as the pair drifted near to him.

"Yes, it is," replied Crocodile sadly. "He is very sick, as you can see."

"I am so sorry, my friend. I wish there was something I could do to help."

The crocodile stopped moving, lying as still in the water as a trapped log. The monkey couldn't help but freeze too.

"But there is, dear friend. This is why I wanted you to come."

"Oh, I will do anything for a good friend like you! I could do a trick, or stand on my head, or fetch him some fruit, perhaps?"

"No," said Crocodile. "That won't be necessary."

"Oh."

"The doctor has told us that there is only one thing in the whole world which will cure my father. And that only you, my dearest, closest friend, can give it to us."

"Tell me! Whatever it is, tell me! I will swing through the jungle from end to end, climb a thousand trees…"

"You don't need to do any of those things!" snapped Crocodile. His father was almost within nosing distance now. The older crocodile opened his bleary eyes and smiled at the monkey, who waved back.

"Hello, Uncle," he shouted cheerily. "What do I need to do then?" he whispered to his friend.

"Oh, not much. Just give me your heart."

Pangolin clapped her claws fully over her eyes and shook her head again and again.

"My – my heart?" said Colobus.

"Yes. Your heart," said his friend, sounding less and less like a friend with every second that passed.

The monkey took a deep breath. He looked at the old crocodile who looked so tired and weak. He looked down at his friend under his feet who looked so sly and dangerous. And his eye was caught by Pangolin, high up on the bank, waving at him and mouthing something.

"What's that?" said Colobus, trying to make out her words. "Show room?"

Pangolin shook her head, and tried miming a paddle, inclining her snout back upriver.

"Go home!" she mouthed again.

"Low dome?" said the monkey.

"Go home!" The pangolin was nearly screaming now.

"Oh, go home!" said Colobus. At last he began to understand that his friend the pangolin was trying to help him.

"Why?" said Crocodile.

Colobus took a deep breath, and focused on the horizon, trying to stay calm. "Yes, I'm so sorry my friend. I wish you had told me before. You see, monkeys..."

He paused, lost for words, and saw Pangolin pointing at her chest, in a mime of carrying a heavy boulder.

"Monkeys are heavy, you see."

"What's that got to do with it?"

The pangolin thumped her chest.

"I mean, our hearts are heavy," said Colobus.

"All the better," said Crocodile, licking his lips.

"Which means..." said the monkey, waving at the pangolin, who was now miming dragging the boulder behind her, straining and heaving, "...that they are too heavy to carry with us." Pangolin nodded encouragement. "They are too heavy, and so we...leave them at home. Yes!" He got it at last. "I would like to give your father my heart, but I have not brought it with me."

"You have to be joking," snarled the huge crocodile under his feet, and the monkey tensed.

"No, I'm not," he squeaked in a higher pitched voice than he meant to. "If you truly need my heart to make your father better, we'll need to go back home and get it."

At which point, time seemed to slow down. Crocodile's father hunched, as if he was getting ready to slide off his rock into the water. Pangolin turned away, unable to watch. And Colobus closed his eyes, waiting for the inevitable. He could feel anger rippling through the monster beneath him. Then –

"Ok, then," said the crocodile. "We'd better go back."

The crocodile's father opened his eyes and began to protest. "No! My son, you're..."

But his son did not listen to him. "He is my friend, Father," he insisted. "If we need his help, we must do what he says."

Now Ma Pangolin turned on her heels as Pa Colobus and Pa Crocodile made their way up river, back to the shore where they first met. She clambered over moss-covered boulders, tramped ferns, and leaped through sprays of red berries to keep pace with the fastest, most powerful animal in the river. Every now and then, as she ran, she would glance anxiously across to the monkey. He caught sight of her, and tried to give a thumbs-up, before remembering that he didn't have any.

Finally, the pair arrived back at the inlet by the milkwood tree, and just as Crocodile was ferrying Colobus into shore, he stopped. His tail came down hard on the monkey, pinning him there.

"Why have you stopped, dear friend, and why are you pinning me down? It hurts."

"Promise me," said the crocodile from beneath the water, which made him sound more frightening than usual.

"Promise you what?"

"That your heart is still on the shore and that you will get it for me."

"I promise with all my, er, heart," said Colobus. "I promise."

Crocodile raised his tail, and his friend jumped for the safety of the shore, clinging to the tree.

He hung there for a moment, his heart going so loud and fast, he wondered that the whole jungle couldn't hear it.

The crocodile could, though.

"Aha!" he called up. "I can hear your heart, my friend. Is that where it is? In that tree?"

"Yes," replied the monkey. "It is. It is in this tree, because I am in this tree, and my heart is in me."

"I don't understand," said Crocodile.

"I am afraid that I was not altogether honest with you, dear friend," said Colobus. "I am afraid that I had my heart with me all the time."

"What?" snarled the crocodile, clambering up onto the shore.

He was an extremely big creature indeed.

"Yes. Because, good friend though you are, I could not let myself be killed to cure your father, much as I would like to! Which isn't much, actually... If you see what I mean."

Crocodile opened his jaws and snapped them with rage, and began leaping and snapping at the monkey, who shot into the branches above. The crocodile scratched at the tree, ripping the white flowers of the milkwood tree into shreds, and the whole jungle quaked at his temper, but nothing he did or said would bring his friend back. Until, at last, when darkness fell upon the water, he slid back in, disappearing from view.

All of these things Ma Pangolin mused upon, as she returned to her little baby pangolins back at home. It had been an exciting and unexpected few days. But she had learned one valuable lesson that she would share with her children as soon as she saw them. It is always a good idea to be wise and cautious, even when dealing with your greatest friends.

It is even better, she suspected, to let your friends think they are the clever ones when, in fact, you are.

Why the Francolin's Legs are Red

Elizabeth Laird

Back in those far off days, the scaly francolin and the tortoise were the best of friends. Ma Tortoise looked just like she does today. She had a hard shell on her back, strong legs with claws on the end, bright eyes like black beads, and a little tail.

Pa Francolin looked nearly the same as he does today. He had the same brown feathers with white edges, the same sharp red beak and the same bright black eyes, just like the tortoise's. But his legs! His legs were not the lovely red colour they are today. They were brown, and nobody looked twice at them.

Pa Francolin liked eating insects. He dug with his sharp beak to pull out delicious fat ones to eat. He liked seeds and nuts, too, and he scratched around with his claws under the kola trees to find them. It was hard work for the francolin to find enough food to eat. He was pecking and scratching, pecking and scratching, all day long.

Ma Tortoise liked to eat leaves, especially the soft juicy ones, as well as blades of grass. It was easy for her to find her food. She just had to stretch out her neck and snatch leaves from the bushes as she passed by, or bend her head and pull at the plants which covered the ground.

Every morning, the francolin and the tortoise went out together to find their food. They helped each other.

"Look!" Francolin called out, in his busy, quick voice. "Nice leaves! Lovely leaves! Big fat juicy leaves for you, Ma Tortoise!"

"Oh – yes – well – thank you very much, Pa Franc-o-lin," Tortoise would reply, in her slow, quiet, dreamy voice. "And look, here's a nut for you, lying on the ground."

And so they passed their days happily together.

One day, Tortoise started talking about the sky. "Just look up there, Pa Francolin!" said Tortoise. "See how blue the sky is. I wish I could fly, like you can. I would like to go up into the sky and see what is there."

Francolin didn't know what to say. He didn't like flying. It was such hard work! It always made him hot and tired. He liked running about on the ground, looking for food and talking to his friend, Ma Tortoise. "There's nothing up there," he said. "Let's talk about something else."

But Tortoise only wanted to talk about the sky. "You must be able to see the whole world from so high up," she said. "Oh please, Pa Francolin, fly up there and tell me what it looks like."

"Not today," Francolin said crossly. "It's too hot."

"But you're such a clever bird, and you've got such beautiful wings," said Tortoise. "I'm sure it will be lovely and cool up in the sky."

"It isn't," Francolin said. "It's hot."

"How do you know if you haven't ever been there?" said

Tortoise.

"I just know," said Francolin. He felt really annoyed with the tortoise now, so he ran on quickly, leaving her behind.

It took a long time for the tortoise to catch up with him. She was looking worried. "Why did you run so fast, Pa Francolin?" she said. "We've come so far from home that I think we're lost."

Francolin looked behind him, and in front of him, and to the left and the right of him. "You're right," he said. "We're lost." He shook his head. He was feeling guilty. "This is all my fault," he said. "I ran on too fast, and left you behind."

"What are we going to do now?" said Tortoise. "It's late in the afternoon, and I'm really hungry. There are no nice green leaves here."

"I'm hungry too," said Francolin. "And I can't see any juicy insects, or delicious seeds to peck. I'm sorry, Ma Tortoise. I really am."

"If you could just fly up to the sky, you could look down and tell us where we are," said Tortoise, who had learned a thing or two from Pa Tortoise.

"Well, I can't," said Francolin. "It's too far."

"There's an ironwood tree over there," said Ma Tortoise, who didn't want to give up. "Could you fly into the tree? Perhaps you will find the way home from up there. Or perhaps you will see a place where there's food for us to eat."

"Oh, all right," said Francolin. He took a deep breath and took off. Flying was such hard work! He beat his wings, and stretched out his neck, and up, up, up he went.

I'm flying! he thought. *It's not so bad. Perhaps I'll do this more often.* He landed on the top of the ironwood tree.

"Well?" Tortoise called up to him. "Can you see the way home?"

"No," said Francolin. "It's getting dark, and there's a mist coming up."

"But can you see anything to eat?" said Tortoise anxiously.

Francolin looked round carefully. "Yes!" he called out. "I can see a palm tree and it's full of nuts. I'll fly across to it and drop them down to you."

So he flew across from one tree to another. *This isn't at all bad,* he told himself. *I'd forgotten that I could fly so well.*

Soon, a nice big pile of palm nuts was lying on the ground under the palm tree. Francolin flew down to the ground again. Tortoise was under the tree already, trying to eat the palm nuts.

"Oh dear, they're too hard. I can't crack them," said Tortoise. "What are we going to do, Pa Francolin?"

Francolin thought for a moment. "We'll have to make a fire to crack the shells," he said. "Come on, Ma Tortoise. Let's get some sticks. We'll have to stay here all night, too, and the fire will keep us warm."

So the tortoise and the francolin collected a big pile of sticks, and they made a fire. Then they put the palm nuts in the hot ashes to roast.

"I think they're ready now," Tortoise said after a while. "I'm going to try one." She pulled a nut out of the hot fire with her hard, horny foot. The shell was easy to crack now. Inside was the delicious soft kernel. "This is lovely," she said. "Why don't you have one, Pa Francolin?"

So the francolin stretched out his beak to pull out a nut. But the nut was in the middle of the fire. He couldn't reach it.

"Do what I do," said Tortoise. "Pull the nuts out with your feet. It's easy! Watch me." And the tortoise put both her front feet in the fire, and slowly pulled out some delicious cooked nuts.

"I can't do that," said Francolin. "Your legs are hard and horny. Mine are much softer. I'll burn myself."

Tortoise thought for a moment. "Why don't you wrap some leaves from the banana plant round your legs to protect them?" she said. "Then you won't get burned."

Francolin was in a hurry now. *If I'm not quick, Ma Tortoise will eat all the nuts and there won't be any left for me,* he thought.

There was a banana plant just nearby. Quickly, the francolin tore down some leaves and wrapped them round his legs. Then, without another thought, he jumped into the fire.

But the leaves didn't help at all! They burned up in a flash, and poor Francolin's legs began to burn too.

"Ow!" he shouted. "Help! I'm on fire!" Flapping his wings and squawking loudly, he managed to run out of the fire. "My legs! My poor legs!" he cried. "Look, Ma Tortoise, they're all red and burned, and I didn't even get any nuts. Oh, how unhappy I am!"

The tortoise felt sorry for the francolin. "Oh dear," she said. "It's my fault. I told you to jump into the fire. Never mind, Pa Francolin. I'll give you half my nuts. Your legs will soon stop hurting. And look, they've turned a lovely red colour. How handsome you look now, Pa Francolin, with your red legs!"

Francolin looked down at himself. "Do you think so, Ma Tortoise? Do I really look nice?" he said.

"Yes," said the tortoise firmly. "You look beautiful. So come and have your supper, Pa Francolin. Then let's go to sleep, and tomorrow we'll find our way home."

So the francolin and the tortoise ate up the nuts together, and went to sleep, and in the morning they walked home. Francolin never learned to fly very high, and Tortoise never talked about the sky again, and they remained the best of friends.

And that is how the francolin's legs turned from a dull, dusty brown to a beautiful, bright red, and he was always very proud of them.

Why the Rat-Mole Stores Groundnuts

Lucy Christopher

Ma Mole, the African pouched rat, sat tight in her hole, cosy and snug. Being a conscientious rat-mole, she had worked hard this past season of dust and heat, collecting nuts from all over the forest and bringing them back in her pouched cheeks to store inside her burrow. Each morning she ran her soft, whiskery snub nose over her hoard as she counted them. Only, Mole wasn't very good at counting.

1, 2,

3, 4, 5…

Mole always forgot what came next.

Mole was better at the subject of Sleeping than Counting. Better, still, at the subject of Eating. Groundnut Munching was her favourite subject of all! Which was just as well, because Mole now had enough groundnuts to last all of the rainy season – more than enough! This made her whiskers twitch with delight.

Like all sensible rodents, Ma Mole knew you could never be too sure about having enough nuts. Perhaps she might get extra hungry one day and eat more than she normally would. Perhaps a friend would come for Groundnuts And Gossiping, and they would feast until their cheeks were round and their bellies big. Perhaps she would remember what number came after 5 and want to count them all. Most of all, though, Ma Mole, like all rat-moles, was a cautious creature. Better to have too many nuts and not eat them all, she thought, then have not nearly enough and go hungry.

Each morning, after she had counted, or tried to count, her hoard of nuts, Mole would burrow up to the sticky-hot surface of the forest and Feel Out The Day. Mole called it Feel Out The Day because that was exactly what she did. Cautiously and shufflingly, Mole would ramble around the rough ground near her burrow entrance, feeling with her sensitive, whiskery skin to see if anything had changed since the day before (and also picking up any more stray nuts or crunchy-tasty crickets while she was there).

As Mole spent so much of her life underground, she had terrible eyesight. In fact, Mole could only see something if it was right in front of her nose, and even then she sometimes mistook the prickly, bad-tempered Pa Porcupine for her good friend Ma Squirrel.

This always gave Mole a nasty shock when she shuffled up to give her soft squirrel friend a hug and found instead Pa Porcupine's sharp spikes and even sharper tongue.

"How many times have I told you, Ma Mole? I look nothing like a giant squirrel, and neither would I want to! Nasty, smelly, squirrely creatures…"

Then prickly Pa Porcupine would shake off Mole's claws with a quiver of dislike, and disappear out of her vision again.

This morning, however, Mole did not hear, or feel, the prickle of Pa Porcupine. Instead, the whole forest was talking. In whispers and squawks and squeals, the animals of the forest gossiped about the humans who lived the other side of the trees.

"They search wider," moaned Guenon.

"Without nuts they have no crops and then they have no food," crowed the crowned eagle.

"They are getting desperate," squeaked Mongoose. "Soon they'll eat us!"

Mole shuffled closer. She squinted and strained, but she could not see beyond the trees to where the humans lived.

"When will they come?" she said.

Mole was scared of the humans; most of the forest animals were. Sometimes, when the humans were hungry, or even when they wanted to play a game, they would catch animals. On one day during the last rainy season, Mole had sat still and silent deep in her burrow as three young humans dug the earth above.

"We'll catch a rat-mole and be hunters," one boy said.

"Catch her by the toe and play," said another.

"We'll feed our bellies!" said the third. "Bring a rat-mole home to roast with plantain!"

That day, Mole had quivered like Pa Porcupine.

Now, she listened as the shrieks became louder in the trees and the whispers rustled the vines. Even the snakes slipped nervously into their dark, hidden places: away.

Soon, Ma Squirrel scampered down from the huge iroko tree above. She shook her bushy tail at Mole and Mole sneezed.

"The drill monkeys are making a plan," Squirrel said. "They say if everyone makes a lot of noise, we will scare the humans away from the forest!"

Mole twitched her whiskers. She knew she was too small to make any noises loud enough to scare away humans; all she could do was bury into her burrow and hide.

Squirrel saw the doubt in Mole's face. She added, "And if that doesn't work, we will race through the trees and lead the humans deep into the forest. There, we will get them lost so they'll never come out."

But Mole could not run fast through the trees, either. She would be caught on the forest floor as soon as she tried.

Mole thought of the nuts hidden in her underground chambers, far more than she could ever eat. If the humans had only managed to find more, like she had… If she hadn't been quite so good at gathering so many…

Mole ground her sharp teeth as she listened to her friend.

Perhaps she could leave out some of her nuts for the humans to find? Then they might not be so hungry and desperate? But, quickly, she remembered how the humans had tried to catch her, and she set her jaw stubbornly. It was up to the humans to find their own nuts. It was their problem if they came into the forest and got scared. Their fault if they got lost, too! And, anyway, a sensible rat-mole should always have more nuts than she needed. It was ancient mole wisdom, after all.

But what if the humans brought their weapons?

What if they did not get scared, or lost?

What if they dug above her hole again and, this time, they did not give up?

It was a lot of thought for one little rat-mole, and it was now past her bedtime. So, Mole hugged Squirrel's soft fur and wished her friend good luck with the plan, then she crawled

down

      down

            deep into her burrow. She dreamed of her mother's warm, sweet milk, and of soft, cool places beneath the earth.

Later, Mole heard noises from the forest. The guenons sneezed an alarm-call and the turacos flapped and shrieked. She heard boom-calls from the drill monkeys, and, further away, the *whee-whaa-whee* of the chimpanzees.

Had the humans come already? Were they in the mood to hunt?

Mole feared the guenon monkeys might be caught first – the bravest and loudest creatures in the forest who would be too proud to hide. Or maybe it might even be Pa Porcupine, who was surely the easiest to catch. Mole, hidden deep in her burrow, might not be caught at all. As Mole quivered, listening to the noises, she felt terribly guilty. Her friends were risking their lives while she did nothing.

It was a long time until the forest quietened. Mole waited to hear the *plip-plop-plip* of the night frogs – her usual alarm clock – but when that didn't come, she dug to the surface anyway.

She was scared

    scared

        scared

            that Ma Squirrel would be gone. Scared, too, that there would be humans waiting above her burrow entrance with big sticks and sharp smiles. But when she reached the surface, all was still.

Cautiously and shufflingly, Mole Felt Out The Night, touching her whiskery snub noise along the ground and sniffing hard. There were broken leaves and chopped vines. There were whispers in the trees, and the smell of chaos.

Perhaps the humans had taken all the animals? Perhaps they were roasting them now over open fires, eating them with spices and smacking their lips? Mole squinted and strained, but even in the dark when her eyesight was usually a little better, she could not see where the humans lived. It was as if every creature in the world had disappeared.

"Ma Squirrel?" she whispered. "Pa Porcupine?"

But the only sounds were the gossiping leaves, and the tiny scuffles from the jumping ants.

Then she felt the hand on her back.

Quickly, she was scooped into the air.

Squeeeeeee, she squeaked.

She waved her claws around wildly, but the human held her firm. Perhaps Mole should play dead – then the human might put her back down and Mole could run for the safety of her burrow. Then Mole realised this was a bad idea – if the human thought Mole were dead, the human might eat her! So Mole struggled harder, kicking out her legs.

Suddenly two huge, brown eyes were very close to Mole, staring right at her.

"Are you lost, little one?" said the human. "You're a rat-mole, aren't you? You're very sweet. Look at your beautiful long whiskers!"

And even though Mole was scared of, and disliked, humans, she could not help but puff her pouched cheeks at the compliment and ruffle her neck fur. This human sounded different to the nasty boys who had tried to dig her from her burrow. This human's voice was softer and lighter. It sounded almost…kind. Mole felt the human stroke, very gently, at the fur underneath her chin. It kind of tickled, though in a nice way. Without meaning to, Mole chirped in pleasure. The human laughed.

"Aren't you lovely," she said. "And all left behind, like me."

It didn't seem, with all this stroking, like this human wanted to eat her. But perhaps that was because she had already eaten all of the other forest animals first! Mole tried to sniff for any signs of this, and, again, she only smelled crushed leaves and broken branches. The human kept stroking under Mole's chin, and, try as she might to stop it, Mole kept chirping. Perhaps some humans weren't so bad.

"Only you and me left, little mole," the human said again. "Everyone else has gone into the trees, searching for food…"

Then, Mole understood. The forest animals' plan had worked – they had led the humans so deep into the forest that they had got lost. Mole felt the girl shiver; as she looked away, her stomach growled. If this human were a mole instead, Mole might have invited her to her burrow for Groundnuts And Gossiping.

Carefully, the human put Mole down. "Go home, little mole," she told her gently. "The hunters will be back soon."

That made Mole's fur bristle but she did not move away, not yet, because even a little rat-mole could tell that this human was sad and scared. And Mole always liked to give comfort to scared animals in the forest; even, she supposed, if they were humans.

Mole settled down into a bundle of juicy taro leaves. From this lower position, Mole could not see the girl, but she could tell where she was by smell and vibration.

"Still here, little one?" The human girl laughed, and again her finger came to stroke under Mole's chin. Mole tilted her head so that the girl could get to that particularly itchy patch that Mole could never scratch by herself.

"I'm called Promise," the girl told Mole. "I'm glad you are here with me on this dark night."

Then Promise told Mole how her father was the best farmer in the village, or how he had been until they had found no more nuts or seeds to sow. She told Mole that it was desperation that had driven them into the forest to look for any food they could find.

"My brother says rat-moles are for catching and eating," Promise said. Mole stiffened when she heard this. "But I don't think that's true. You're too cute and kind. You're brave too, to sit here with me. The bravest animal in the forest!"

But Promise had this wrong. The other forest animals had been the brave ones, leading away the hunters while Mole had stayed hidden.

"I don't like hunting," Promise said. She settled into the leaves too, resting up against the ebony tree. "I said we should search for nuts and seeds here, on the edge of the trees, but my father said there was no use. So, I said I would wait behind and search while they hunted. But I haven't found anything yet, and now it is dark, and they haven't come back. Maybe they won't come back at all…"

Her voice trailed away.

Mole felt a warm, salty tear land softly onto her fur. Quickly, she scooted back into her burrow with an idea. She went

    down,

        down,

            down to where all her nuts were hidden. She took as many as she could in her cheeks and carried them up to the girl.

Promise laughed when she saw them, marvelling at the mole. "For me? You knew what I wanted?"

This time, when Promise stroked her, the rat-mole tilted her chin the other way so that Promise could reach her second most itchy spot.

"But don't you need these nuts?" Promise asked. "The rains can go on for many months!"

In answer, Mole went back into the burrow and brought up more, and some seeds too. Eventually, Mole brought up enough nuts and seeds for Promise to feed her whole family – enough to plant crops for the village, too. And still Mole had nuts to spare for herself. Promise counted them out, and Mole finally learned the numbers that came after five. There were a lot of them.

"But why would you want to help us?" Promise asked.

Again, Mole thought of how the boys had tried to hunt her from her burrow. She nuzzled a nut towards Promise's feet, and looked towards the deepest part of the forest. Perhaps, Mole thought, with enough nuts and seeds for crops, the hunters would no longer want to hunt her friends. No longer want to hunt her! Ma Mole tried to squeak this to Promise, tried to make her understand.

"You are a clever little mole," Promise nodded slowly. "I will bring these nuts to my family and tell them never to hunt the forest animals again."

Carefully and shufflingly, Promise and Mole went into the forest. Mole squeaked to lead Promise on, and Promise dropped nuts behind them in a trail so that they could find their way out again.

But deep, deep, in the forest's heart was a dangerous scene. The humans were bunched tight in a clearing and, high above in the trees, the forest animals shrieked and threw things at their hunters. The humans had sharp sticks pointed at Mole's friends: the animals were trapped. When Mole realised this, she shrilled and squeaked loudly. Promise ran into the clearing.

"Stop!" she shouted. She did not seem scared at all.

"She's carrying a rat-mole," cried one of the hunters.

"She's brought us food!" said another.

A third human moved to grab Mole, but Promise tucked Mole safe inside her clothing, close to her body. "You'll not hurt this mole!"

Quickly, Promise explained. "This rat-mole has saved us. She has given us some of her own nuts and seeds so that we can grow crops to eat and sell. We do not have to hunt these animals now."

And, slowly and curiously, the humans listened. Could it be that a rat-mole had been kind to them? But why? The humans had hunted rat-moles like this one for as long as they could remember.

As Promise spoke to the humans, Mole squeaked to the animals in the trees. She told them of the plan she had made with Promise. It went like this: each dry season, Mole would gather nuts for the humans as well as for herself, and she would scatter some of these nuts around the edge of her burrow for the humans to collect. In turn, the humans would no longer hunt the forest animals.

"Ingenious idea!" cried a drill.

"A marvellous mole," said Guenon.

"You stopped us being roasted!" shouted Squirrel.

Even Pa Porcupine quivered his grudging gratitude.

The animals swung from the branches in delight, while the humans below cowered in the rain of falling leaves. But the humans smiled, too. For here was a solution. They would have crops. They would make money selling these crops and nuts at the market. They would not go hungry.

"But no one is to dig out any more rat-moles," Promise told the humans. "Not even if you find it fun!" She wagged a finger at the boys sternly.

Mole tilted her head for another scratch.

"You really did save us, little rat-mole," Promise whispered.

But Mole knew that Promise had saved her, too. Without Promise, Mole would never have learned that being brave and considerate, even to those she was scared of, meant that everyone, really, was saved.

And so it was that each year, when the humans searched for nuts, they would always pay a visit to Ma Mole's burrow. There, in the dug up dirt on the edge of the forest, they would find what Mole had left for them: scattered nuts, and the seeds they needed for their crops. And they no longer hunted the forest animals.

And, somewhere deep

                deep

                              deep underground, Mole would twitch her whiskers happily, knowing that everyone had delicious groundnuts for their bellies, and friends to share them with. And that, Mole knew, was the most important thing of all.

Why the Tortoise Eats Mushrooms

Gill Lewis

Sometimes change happens in the silence between heartbeats. Sometimes it follows in the footsteps of strangers. But sometimes change comes blowing in on the wind.

Ma Elephant was the first to feel it.

The old elephant lifted her trunk to the sky and tasted dust and heat in the air. "Animals of Korup," she called. Her voice rumbled across the forest. "Animals of Korup, listen to me. Although our world is bright and new, I feel a great change is coming."

The animals stopped what they were doing. The buffalo lifted her head from the Mana river, the cool water dripping from her lips. The bush pig stopped rootling in the ground and shook the soil from his snout. The drill monkey and the chimpanzee put down the fruits they were munching, and the hornbill settled on a branch, turning his head from side to side, to hear what Ma Elephant had to say. She was the oldest and wisest of them all. Even Man stopped to listen.

"Animals of Korup," called Ma Elephant in a voice as deep as the earth. "It is a fierce and cruel wind that blows. It will bring months of sun and no rain. The dry season will last longer than it ever has before. We are in for hard times. The corn will shrivel and blacken on their stalks and the cassava will wilt upon the ground. The rivers will run dry. We must work together to collect food for the harvest. There is no time to lose. If we work together, we may survive."

The animals set out at once. The turacos and hornbills collected seeds and nuts from the tallest trees. The bees offered their wild honey. The bush pig dug up yams and the buffalo collected the ripened corn. The porcupine speared berries on the tips of her sharp quills, and the chimpanzee and the drill monkey picked armfuls of kola fruit. The animals piled the harvested food beneath the bush mango tree.

Ma Elephant flapped her huge ears and nodded. "Well done everyone, but we must hurry if we are to have enough food to see us through the months ahead."

The animals worked harder and faster, stripping the umbrella trees of fruit and pulling root crops from the soil. They lay corncobs on the ground to ripen in the sun.

Meanwhile, Man ran around the forest collecting stones.

"Tsk, what are you doing?" said Ma Elephant. "We cannot eat stones."

Man looked at Ma Elephant with sly eyes. "Oh, Aunty," he said, "I thought they were roots we could eat."

"You fool," barked the drill monkey.

"Idiot," chattered the mongoose.

"You must help with the harvest," scolded Ma Elephant. "Soon dust and heat will be upon us."

Man watched Ma Elephant walk away, swinging her trunk

from side to side. He smiled to himself. He had a plan. If he kept all the food for himself then he would survive. He was the cleverest animal and he would show them all.

As the sun sank lower in the sky, all the animals settled down for the night. They were exhausted but happy. The harvest was safely gathered. Their hard work had been rewarded. They all slept so soundly that they didn't hear Man hurrying back and forth with stones in the small dark hours. All through the night, Man built a wall. He encircled it around the bush mango tree and the harvested food. He built the wall higher and higher, until he could not see over the top of it.

When the sun rose the next day, it burned hot and fierce.

The animals woke up, blinking their eyes in the bright light. They stared at the strange new construction in their forest. Man sat on top of his wall, looking down at them.

"Where is our food?" demanded the bush pig. "What have you done with it?"

"You will have to collect more," said Man. "This is my food now. Everything inside this wall belongs to me."

"But we harvested it," squealed the civet. "It is for us all to share."

"Then you should have been more careful where you left it," sneered Man.

"What have you done?" roared the buffalo. "This is food for our children. How will they survive?"

"You have cheated us," called out the bushbuck. "We gathered the food together."

"You're a trickster," whistled the turaco.

"We'll get our food back," screeched the drill monkey and the chimpanzee.

They began to climb the wall, but Man threw rocks at them and drove them back down.

"This is my wall, my food," shouted Man. "You were too stupid helping each other. I am cleverer than you all."

"We'll fly in and take the fruit," called the birds. They flew high in the sky, preparing to swoop down, but Man placed more stones on the walls, curving them inwards, creating a roof above him. Man sealed himself within a dome of stones.

The drill monkey drummed his fists against the roof. The buffalo heaved her great shoulder against the walls. But Man had built his domed house so strong that none of the animals could break it down.

"Man!" ordered Ma Elephant. "Come out at once."

Man removed one stone from the bottom of his house and stuck his head out. "Go away all of you," he shouted. "This is my house, my food. Go and find your own."

"But these forests belong to all of us," cried the animals. "Our young ones need to eat."

"That is your problem, not mine," snapped Man.

Ma Elephant swung her great trunk from side to side. "Oh Man," she sighed. "What have you done? You will have food for one season only."

"Rubbish!" screamed Man. "I have a bush mango tree in

here. I have a pool of clear water. I have everything I need."

Ma Elephant flapped her ears and shook her head. "But how will your soil be nourished if Buffalo cannot spread her droppings on the ground? How will the seeds be dispersed if there are no birds to carry them? How will your flowers be pollinated if there are no bees? How will your tree grow if there is no light?"

"Pah!" said Man. "I don't need you. I don't need the forest. I have food for a lifetime. I am cleverer than you all." He pulled his head inside his home and sat in the darkness munching sweet mangoes, feeling very pleased with himself indeed.

Outside, the sky was blue and cloudless.

Days turned into weeks.

The sun burned down, turning the grass from green to brown, and wilting leaves upon the trees. The ground became hard and cracked and thirsty for rain that did not come. The riverbeds of the Akpasang, the Mana and the Korup became dust-dry where water had once flowed. The animals roamed the fields and forests scraping for any morsels of food they could find. They became rib-thin. Their coats lost their shine and their eyes sunk deep into their sockets. In the heat of the day, they could barely move to flick away the flies that bothered them.

Only Man had enough to eat and drink. He watched the other animals turn to skin and bone, while he feasted on the store of food and drank from the pool of cool water.

Inside his house of stones, Man smiled at his

cleverness.

The animals passed by and asked for food. Their young were listless and weak.

"Please," implored the chimpanzee, holding her baby for man to see. "Please may I have a little of your food, so that my baby can live."

Man peered out at her. His food store was now running low and he might not have enough to share. "Go away," he shouted. "You should have guarded your food more carefully, and not wasted time helping each other."

Weeks turned into months and still the sun beat relentlessly upon the earth. Even Man began to feel hungry. He had eaten all the fruit and yams, but he had his corn to eat. The pool of water had turned to mud, but if he dug deep into the soil he had just enough to drink.

Meanwhile, the animals tried to rest in the shadows on the sun-scorched earth. They were so weary that only Ma Elephant noticed the first threads of white drifting high across the sky and curling around the tip of Mount Yuhan. She reached up her trunk to taste the air. "Animals, animals," she trumpeted loudly. "Look up, look up! For rain is coming."

Above them, huge clouds began to unfurl over the land. Raindrops slid from the sky, slowly at first, hissing as they hit the hot soil. Then rain fell faster and faster, quenching the earth and filling the dry riverbeds.

The animals danced in the rain. The buffalo and bushbuck kicked up their hooves in the wide puddles. The birds preened

the dust from their feathers until their colours shone bright and new. The chimpanzees and monkeys screeched and hooted for joy. The grass grew up fast beneath their feet, bright, vivid and green. Leaves unfurled upon the trees and new buds burst into flower.

Life had returned to Korup.

Man stuck his head out through the hole at the bottom

of his house of stones and saw the animals filling their bellies with lush grass and forest fruits. His mouth watered. He tried to reach out for a handful of wild celery, but the buffalo stamped her foot on the ground.

"You did not share your food with us," Buffalo snorted, "so why should we share ours with you?"

The chimpanzee jumped down from her tree and aimed a stone at Man, sending him scuttling back inside. "You said you didn't need the forest. You said you were the cleverest animal of us all."

"And I am," screeched Man, in frustration. "I have more than enough in here. I don't need any of you." Man gnashed his teeth. He had eaten the last of his food. Only a few mouldy seeds and nuts remained.

Ma Elephant stopped by to visit. She scratched her large bottom against the walls of his house. "How are you Man? Are you hungry yet?"

"Me?" snapped Man. "Of course not. I am too clever for that. I have food to last a lifetime."

Ma Elephant went on her way, humming to herself. Inside his house, Man's stomach ached with emptiness. But what could he eat? The bush mango tree no longer bore leaves or fruit. It stood in the middle of his house, a dead thing, and a reminder of what he had lost. Man was so hungry that he boiled stones to eat, but he broke his teeth as he tried to crunch on them. The pool of water had become stinking and brown. It was so dark and damp inside his house that only mushrooms grew. Man chewed on them, mashing them between his toothless gums.

Months turned into years, and Man stayed inside his house of stones. His mouth became hard and beaklike from eating only mushrooms. His skin became thickened and wrinkled from the damp air. Once long and lean, his limbs became bent and stumpy from crouching beneath the low stone roof. His eyes were small and squinty from peering in the darkness all day.

The other animals ignored him. But every so often, Ma Elephant would stop by. "Hey ho, Man," she would call. She pushed her trunk through the small hole at the bottom of Man's house. "Have you enough to eat?"

"Plenty," snapped Man, chewing on a mushroom. "The tree blossoms every day and bears fine fruit. The water runs clear and there are plenty of fish. I have everything I need. I don't need you. I am the cleverest of you all."

"That is good to hear," said Ma Elephant, smiling to herself. "To be clever is a fine thing indeed."

Man watched the other animals from inside his house of stones. The bush pig grunted in pleasure as he wallowed in his mud-bath. The buffalo grazed the fresh grass, while the calves bounded and played in the forest clearings. The monkeys swung hand and tail through the trees. The branches hung low, laden with more fruit than the animals could eat. Man's mouth watered at the sweet smell and at the sound of water rushing in the river. His heart ached to be part of the forest once more.

One day he could bear it no longer.

"Ma Elephant!" He called. "I miss the forest and the animals. I miss the fine food and the water that runs clear."

The other animals stopped to listen.

"But you have everything you need," insisted the bush pig.

"Why do you want our food when you have plenty of your own?" barked the drill monkey.

Ma Elephant knelt down in the dirt so that she could look Man in the eye. "What is it you want?"

Man stuck his head out of his hole. "I want to run through the forests without this burden of stones. I want to see the sky. I want to eat the wild fruits and drink from the clear water."

"Then come out," smiled Ma Elephant. "If we share this forest, there is plenty of food for everyone. It is only your pride that is stopping you now."

Man tried to squeeze out of his house of stones, but he had lived so long beneath his burden that the stones had become part of him.

"Help me, Aunty," he pleaded.

Ma Elephant tried to crush the stones beneath her foot, but not even she could break them. She heaved her great trunk against Man's house, and lifted the house of stones clear from the ground. "You will have to walk with your house of stones upon your back," sighed Ma Elephant. "I can do no more."

Man tried. With his stumpy legs, he could only manage a slow shuffle forward. His toothless beak was too weak to bite into the fresh fruit. When he opened his small eyes, the light was too bright to see. His stony house had become a heavy shell upon his back. "What has become of me?" wailed Man. "What sort of creature am I?"

"A liar," squeaked the hyrax.

"A cheat," said the civet.

"From now on we will call you Tortoise," said the drill. "And everyone will see the burden you carry on your back and recognise you for the trickster you are."

"No!" cried Man. "How has this happened? Tell me, Aunty, am I not the cleverest animal?"

Ma Elephant nodded her head. "You are indeed the cleverest animal. You imagine and dream. You invent and build. There is no other creature like you."

"Then why," said Man, "why am I living alone, eating only mushrooms?"

Ma Elephant flapped her huge ears. "Man," she sighed. "To be clever is indeed a fine thing, but without wisdom, it can destroy you and everything else around you. It makes you the most dangerous animal of all."

Man wept salt tears, realising the creature he had become. "But can I change from this? Is it possible?"

Ma Elephant sighed so deeply, even the trees seem to hear. "Maybe," she said. "Maybe. But one day, there will be many more of your kind on this earth, and each will have to make the choice between living in darkness, or walking out into the light."

"But how do we change?" asked Man, desperate for her answer.

Ma Elephant swung her trunk from side to side. "You must give back to the forest. You will have to undo what you have done."

"And will it be enough?" said Man.

Ma Elephant smiled at him. "No," she said gently. "To become human again, you must first open your heart."

Man watched Ma Elephant turn to leave. Could he change? Had he left it too late? He began to wonder if indeed it could be possible. He began to imagine and to dream. He thought of the chimpanzee baby that had needed his help. He thought of the birds, and how they lit up the dark canopy of leaves with their bright colours. He thought of all the creatures that shared Korup and how he was one of them, not separate. He closed his eyes and listened to the beating of his heart, and as he did so, he felt a glow of warmth deep inside his chest spreading outwards to the very tips of his fingers and his toes. His limbs grew long and lean again. The stones on his back began to shift and drop away.

"Look Aunty, look!" Man shouted. "See…it is happening…"

For the first time in a long, long while, the corners of his mouth stretched wide across his face, and Man began to smile.

Ma Elephant stopped at the forest edge. Her deep voice rumbled through the earth. "Then come with me, Man. We are waiting for you."

Sometimes change happens in the silence between heartbeats. Sometimes it follows in the footsteps of strangers. But sometimes change comes blowing in on the wind.

BIOGRAPHIES

Emmie van Biervliet
Emmie is a mixed media artist whose work has a dreamlike quality, with magical realism an integral part of it. When possible she works in situ in art residencies – say an abandoned building in Havana, a cave in Cappadocia or a car crossing the Atacama Desert. She works with a number of galleries and exhibits regularly in the UK and internationally.

Lucy Christopher
Lucy is the best-selling and international award-winning author of *Stolen*, *Flyaway* and *The Killing Woods*. She works as Senior Lecturer in Creative Writing at Bath Spa University, where she has a PhD in Creative Writing. Lucy has co-written the screen adaptation of *Stolen*, and is finishing her fourth novel.

Abi Elphinstone
Abi Elphinstone grew up in Scotland where she spent her childhood running wild across highland glens. After being coaxed out of her tree house, she studied English at university then became a teacher. Now she writes books (*The Dreamsnatcher*, *The Shadow Keeper*) and travels the world looking for stories.

Adèle Geras
Adèle published her first book in 1976 and has since written more than 100 books for young readers of all ages as well as several novels for adults. *Troy* was Highly Commended for the Carnegie Medal. When she was very young she lived in Nigeria and has also spent time in the Gambia and Tanzania.

Elizabeth Laird
Elizabeth is the multi-award-winning author of many successful children's & young adult novels. She has lived all over the world: Malaysia, India, Iraq, Austria, Ethiopia and New Zealand. Her travels have undeniably influenced her style of writing and

choice of topics, and she is well known for tackling a wide range of global issues through her work.

Sarah Lean
As a child, Sarah wanted to be a writer and dictated stories to her mother, until she bought a laptop of her own several years ago and decided to type them herself. Her fascination with animals began when she was aged eight and a stray cat decided to adopt her.

Gill Lewis
Gill Lewis writes stories for children inspired by her love of the natural world and from her work as a vet. Her books have been translated into many languages and have won international awards for environmental literature.

Geraldine McCaughrean
Geraldine has written 170 books and been published in 50 countries. She even won the chance to write a sequel to *Peter Pan* for Great Ormond Street Hospital. She loves writing picture books, adult novels and everything in between. It beats working! And people even give her prizes for it, like the Carnegie Medal.

Tom Moorhouse
Tom Moorhouse is a strange hybrid being, half children's author and half research ecologist (an entity probably not called an "authologist"). His books to date are all animal fiction, including the award-winning *The River Singers*, its sequel *The Rising* and *Trickster*, which is the world's only "ratrospective".

Beverley Naidoo
Beverley was born in South Africa where she came to love animal tales as a child. However, humans rather than animals pose the greatest dangers in her early novels like *Journey to Jo'burg* and *No Turning Back*. After a feisty Tortoise crept into her Carnegie-winning *The Other Side of Truth*, she has regularly returned to the tales of her youth.

Ifeoma Onyefulu

Ifeoma's first child inspired her to start writing for children – there were very few books about Africans at the time. She has since written 23 books, won several awards, including the Children's Africana Book Award twice, and been nominated for a Kate Greenaway Medal. She is also a photographer and has exhibited at the British Museum and the Afrika Center in Norway.

Piers Torday

Piers Torday is the author of the *Last Wild* trilogy, which has sold around the world and won the Guardian Children's Fiction Prize. His latest book for children is *There May Be A Castle*. Unfortunately, he is still not as clever as a certain pangolin.

About Lantana Publishing

Lantana's mission is to select the best of diverse writing from around the world, working with prize-winning authors and illustrators from many countries. Lantana's acclaimed cross-cultural collaborations have won the Children's Africana Best Book Award, made it onto the White Ravens honour list, and been nominated for a Kate Greenaway Medal. Lantana is proud to bring UK children's publishing one step closer towards achieving a more diverse and inclusive children's book landscape for the next generation of young readers.

ACKNOWLEDGEMENTS

It feels strange to tell you about a place I have never visited. Korup, in Cameroon, is exotic for me. It has beautiful rainforest, amazing wildlife, and a national park entered by a rope-bridge, hanging high above white rapids. It is a place with incredibly rich and varied stories. I have never been there, but maybe that doesn't matter.

You don't have to have been to Korup to understand that life there can be hard. You can imagine a school where there is only one textbook, or a home where the only printed words are on an old poster. You can understand that education beyond primary level is reserved for those who can send children and money to relatives in larger towns. You can imagine what happens when stories are forgotten and the animals who throng those stories become just a way of earning an income, from hunting.

We all know what good a book, in the right hands at the right time, can do. That's why we wrote *A Wisp of Wisdom*. We wrote it because it will help – perhaps only a little, but it will help. Thanks to the generosity of the crowdfunders who backed us, at least 2,000 children in Korup will have a copy of the book you are holding. They have something to read. They will know their stories. It's a small thing, but a good thing. Thank you.

This book exists because of the guys who work in Korup. They started this. They collected the stories. And, fittingly, they will return them. Christos Astaras, Robinson Diotoh Orume, Malenoh Sewuh Ndimbe and other members of the Korup Rainforest Conservation Society are doing amazing work in the region, and together with the ever-wonderful Wildlife Conservation Research Unit, Oxford University, are handling the logistics of getting our book printed in Cameroon and distributing it to the children who need it.

Massive thanks also go to Liz Cross for all of her

encouragement, feedback and support – right from the book's inception – and to the brilliant Story Museum, and the members of the Cameroon Forum.

Authors. Strange people. I don't know of many other professionals who, when asked to give their expertise for free, would agree quite so enthusiastically. Except for illustrators, of course, and namley Emmie van Biervliet, our amazing artist. That any of you went along with this idea still strikes me as bizarre, and wonderful. Thank you all.

Beyond such trifles as the creation of stories and art, a staggering amount of work and talent goes into making a book: the editing, the layout, the design, the paper, the cover, the colours...the list of tasks, considerations and decisions goes on (and on, and on). That Alice Curry and Caroline Godfrey and the Lantana team accepted this challenge, and went on to produce this book, is simply incredible. I can't thank you enough for taking on this project and seeing it through.

You have all been spectacular.

Tom Moorhouse

Pangolin

By Piers Torday

You must never call it a pan-go-thing
For that is not the song to sing.
And also not a pan-go-thin
(He'd be the first to raid your biscuit tin).
He cannot dance or play the mandolin,
Instead he likes to curl or go a-burrowing
In armoured scales that could befit a king
- Of earth, of root, of tree -
A sight to see, this shy and bright-eyed majesty,
This wondrous thing,
This pan-go-lin.